THE WRITINGS OF

WILL ROGERS

I - 1

SPONSORED BY

The Will Rogers Memorial Commission
and Oklahoma State University

ROGERS CHRONOLOGY

1879, November 4   Born at the Rogers Ranch, near Claremore, Indian Territory

1887-1898   Academic Training: Drumgoole School, near Chelsea, Presbyterian Mission School, Tahlequah; Harrell Institute, Muskogee; Willie Halsell College, Vinita (1892-1896), all in Indian Territory; Scarritt Collegiate Institute, Neosho, Missouri; Kemper Military School, Boonville, Missouri

1898-1902   Ranching Activities: After leaving Kemper, Rogers worked on Ewing Ranch, Higgins, Texas, and later managed Rogers ranch in Indian Territory

1902-1903   Will Rogers began his show career in South Africa with Texas Jack's Wild West Show as "The Cherokee Kid," and toured Australia and New Zealand in Wirth Brothers Circus

1904-1915   Rogers returned to the United States in 1904 and was with the Mulhall Wild West Show at St. Louis World's Fair, and in Madison Square Garden, New York, in 1905. From 1905-1915 he appeared on the vaudeville circuit in the United States, Canada, and three times in Europe

1908, November 25   Rogers married Betty Blake of Rogers, Arkansas

1912-1926   Rogers played many roles on stage and screen, including Ziegfeld's *Midnight Frolic;* Ziegfield Follies (1916-1925); first motion picture, *Laughing Bill Hyde* (1918); and later made motion pictures for Goldwyn (1919-1921), and Roach (1923-1924)

1916-1925   Early series of writings: Rogers began his newspaper efforts; *The Cowboy Philosopher on the Peace Conference* (1919); *The Cowboy Philosopher on Prohibition* (1919); syndicated Convention Articles (1920-1932); Syndicated Weekly Articles (1920-1935); *The Illiterate Digest* (1924); and syndicated "The Worst Story I've Heard Today" (1925-1927)

1919	The family moved to California, where Rogers had signed film contracts with Goldwyn
1922-1935	During these years Will Rogers spoke on radio (including sponsored broadcasts, 1930-1935) ; and traveled widely, appearing at banquets, and on lecture tours (1925-1928)
1926-1935	Rogers wrote many of his magazine articles during this period for the *Saturday Evening Post* (1926-1932) ; *Life* (1928) ; and *American Magazine* (1929-1930)
1926-1935	Later series of writings: *Letters of a Self-Made Diplomat to His President* (1926) ; syndicated Daily Telegrams (1926-1935) ; *There's Not a Bathing Suit in Russia and Other Bare Facts* (1927) ; *Ether and Me, or "Just Relax"* (1929)
1926	Significant events during this period were Rogers' European tour with his family where he played in the *Cochran Revue,* London. While abroad he made motion pictures including *Tip-Toes* and a series *Strolling Through Europe With Will Rogers.* Finally he performed at benefits for Irish theater victims, and upon returning home, played benefits for Florida hurricane sufferers. Because of his contributions to and interest in the people of this country, Californians in Beverly Hills designated him honorary mayor
1927-1935	Later motion picture and stage roles: Rogers made his last silent film, *A Texas Steer* (1927) ; appeared in a musical comedy *Three Cheers* (1928-1929) ; his first talking film, *They Had to See Paris* (1929) ; and the stage play *Ah Wilderness* (1934)
1927	Significant events in 1927: Rogers spoke at benefit performances for victims of Mississippi River flood; suffered serious illness and surgery; was designated "Congressman-at-Large for the United States of America," by the National Press Club, Washington; and visited Mexico at the invitation of Ambassador Dwight W. Morrow
1928	Significant events in 1928: Rogers visited the Pan-American Conference, Havana, and talked of his mock candidacy for President on the Anti-Bunk Party ticket

1930-1935	Later international visits: Rogers attended the London Disarmament Conference (1930) ; visited Nicaragua (1931) ; in East Asia (1931-1932) ; Latin America (1932) ; and went on a round-the-world tour (1934)
1935, August 15	Rogers died with Wiley Post in an airplane crash near Point Barrow, Alaska

Doc left me the map of the operation — Looks simple, don't it?

ETHER AND ME

OR

"Just Relax"

BY

WILL ROGERS

Edited with an Introduction by
Joseph A. Stout, Jr.

OKLAHOMA STATE UNIVERSITY PRESS
Stillwater, Oklahoma
1973

Note to scholars: The Putman's book, the original illustrations and drawings, and the author's original manuscript are reproduced with permission of the Will Rogers Memorial Commission, Claremore, Oklahoma, and The Rogers Company, Beverly Hills, California. The scholarly apparatus and notes to the texts of Rogers' works as they appear in this volume are copyrighted and the usual rules about the use of copyrighted material apply.

(Second Printing)

International Standard Book Number 0-914956-01-9

Library of Congress Catalog Number 73-79456

Printed in the United States of America

INTRODUCTION

"Dear Will, All I know is what I read in the papers and I see that your Gall isnt what it used to be. Hope you wont be disappointed in the scar and that they didnt take any of the funny part out of you." Thus wrote E. C. Romfh, a concerned friend, when he heard of the humorist's gallstone operation. Actually people throughout the world sent telegrams expressing their anxiety for Rogers' condition. He had always enjoyed vigorous health, and constantly was concerned about his fellow man, whether ill or financially destitute. Rogers refused at any time to allow his personal discomfort to slow his pace. Once, while speaking in Bluefield, Virginia, Rogers suffered severe pains from the gallstones, but traveled on to New Orleans to help raise money for flood victims. Then in 1927, as he was traveling from one speaking engagement to another, the cowboy philosopher suffered the most severe attack he had ever experienced. He stopped to rest in Oklahoma briefly before going home to California, but by the time he reached Beverly Hills he was miserable.

Realizing that Rogers was in even more pain than he would admit, his wife Betty immediately called Dr. Percy G. White, the family physician. Dr. White examined the patient, and called in his associate, Dr. E. Clarence Moore. These two men operated one of the best clinics in the United States, and after more examination White, a specialist in internal medicine, and Moore, a surgeon, concluded that Will suffered gall bladder trouble and an operation was necessary. The patient protested—but not too loudly, for he was in considerable pain. He also had other problems, for the night he was sent to the hospital he was scheduled to address a benefit banquet to raise money for a new gym at Occidental College. However, Betty promised to appear in his place, and take along William S. Hart to speak to the group. Rogers was relieved when Hart consented to speak, for he considered it his duty to fulfill his obligations regardless of conditions. With all seemingly settled and on his way to the operating room, he dictated a telegram to Mrs. Rogers telling perhaps himself to "Relax, lie perfectly still and relax."

Even when facing major surgery, Will Rogers found humor in his predicament. He blamed his stomach trouble on "Home Cooking," for he said he was so accustomed to eating in restaurants that his stomach no longer could tolerate home cooked meals. Only if he could eat at different places would his stomach be fooled and cease to cause him pain. While he joked, however, the national press speculated endlessly about the cause of his illness. New York papers theorized that Rogers suffered acute indigestion. Others insisted the problem was appendicitis, but Will said he knew all along the pain was in the wrong place for the appendix.

While in the hospital, both before and after his surgery, Rogers continued to produce his daily telegrams and weekly articles. In fact, he wrote several telegrams to be released during his first few days of confinement, hoping not to miss too many. Just before the operation he wrote, "Well, here comes the wagon. I do hope my scar will not suffer in size with other, older and more experienced scars." And, although seriously ill for several days afterwards, he still found humor in his situation. Writing Charles A. Lindbergh a public telegram inviting him to Beverly Hills, Will added: "P. S. just saw the scar. If they charge by the inch, that operation will be the serious one." Like most hospital patients, Will complained about the food, reminding his readers, "I sure do like my chili. If I could have just bogged down a few bowls of good old greasy chili, I would have been well in a week." Operations were not his only concern, he also wrote of United States participation in the recent world disarmament conference. Critical of American destruction of shipping and a national willingness to appease the Japanese, Rogers insisted that "We just sunk till we had nothing else to sink." Only on Monday, June 20, 1927, did Rogers fail to send his telegram to the McNaught Syndicate.

He returned home three weeks after entering the hospital. His doctors ordered him to rest, but nothing could keep him down long. Almost immediately he began his vigorous writing schedule. As a joke he wrote in one of his telegrams that he would give a reward to the first person from Claremore, Oklahoma, to arrive in Beverly Hills. The trip had to be made in a Ford—and made without stops. After paying off the first three who completed the trip. Will was forced to withdraw his offer; it was costing him far more than the joke was worth. Yet it kept his mind off his operation, and in that respect was a welcome diversion.

Will Rogers had been providing considerable diversion for others for a long time. He was born on his father's ranch near what became Oologah, Indian Territory, November 4, 1879. The ranch had been in the Rogers family since 1856, and remained so until 1961, when the United States government obtained most nearby territory for the construction of Oologah Dam. Rogers grew up around cattle, horses, and men who worked the range; he loved Oklahoma and intended to retire near his birthplace. Part Cherokee, he took to riding naturally, and began developing his roping skills at an early age. His formal education started in a one room school house at Drumgoole near Chelsea; thereafter he attended several schools in Oklahoma and Missouri. While at Scarritt College in Neosho, Missouri, Will improved his rope tricks, and once even roped an old mare owned by a teacher. The horse pulled the rope away and stampeded, her colt following, across the tennis courts and through the streets of Neosho. At the school, Rogers apparently did satisfactory work, but returned home just before the first term ended, probably as a result of the death of his brother-in-law. Home only briefly, his father sent him to Kemper Military School at Boonville, Missouri, hoping that strict discipline would prompt him to work harder at his studies. After remaining at the academy a year, Will left school for the last time. He worked briefly on a ranch in Texas, and eventually owned his own stock on the family ranch in Indian Territory. However, he soon tired of ranching, sold his stock, and began traveling widely. His great skill with a lariat took him to dozens of foreign countries, to Wild West shows, to the Ziegfeld Follies, and into movies by 1919.

The decade of the twenties saw him become America's best-known actor, journalist, political commentator, and humorist. As such, he reflected his era, and reading his telegrams, weekly articles, and books and or listening to his speeches provides one of the best insights to an understanding of the first three decades of the twentieth century. An astute political analyst, he was often pragmatic, and his cogent comments about the activities of the government and its leaders both enlightened Americans and provided them with an opportunity to laugh at themselves. Sometimes Rogers was critical, but always his remarks were made in a lighthearted way. He had strong beliefs about society and the relationship of men and countries. Likewise, he believed it necessary for a country to re-examine itself constantly. Even more significantly, he voiced insights into American society in a way every person could understand.

Ether and Me or "Just Relax" is the story of his operation. First serialized in the *Saturday Evening Post* of November 5 and 12, 1927, under the title "A Hole in One," the story drew wide attention and many chuckles. He had suggested "Scarbelly" be the title, but *Post* editors obviously thought this inappropriate. They also made some stylistic changes in the published version of the manuscript. When G. P. Putnam's Sons published it in book form, little additional editing was necessary. The volume sold extremely well. In fact, G. P. Putman's Sons reprinted the book twelve times, beginning in 1935 with the memorial edition. Almost eighty thousand copies had sold by 1956. Additional impressions were printed by the Rogers family, and even more copies sold than the original publisher recorded.

This new volume presents for the first time the original manuscript as Will sent it to the *Post*. His correction, annotations, and style are clearly evident. Rogers had a natural style; in fact, despite his travels throughout the world, he continued to write much as he did when he began his career. In this volume no attempt has been made to edit either of the two versions of the work. Where textual differences exist and significant changes occur, the *Post* version has been noted. The illustrations in the original *Post* articles were by Herbert Johnson; the drawings in the Putnam's book were by Grim Natwick.

When the Putnam's book appeared in 1929, almost every newspaper in the country reviewed it. The *New York Times,* although somewhat disappointed, hastened to add that the book was funniest when Will Rogers was "describing his sensations under ether. Not because of the ether, or the gallstones, or the doctors, or the wrestlers who have been hired to hold him down, but because he employs his ether dream to comment on events of national import." The *Los Angeles Times* commented that Will tried to make the reader "understand that the purpose of the story is to pay the doctor bill. Let's all help by buying the book! It's worth the dollar and the pictures by Grim Natwick are thrown in free." Generally the reviewers recommended its purchase.

Will Rogers became a close friend of Doctors White and Moore, and certainly believed the operation had been worthwhile, for a few years later he sent a telegram to a convention of the medical profession in Santa Barbara in which he expressed regret that he could not be there to speak, but told them, "Anyhow have a drink on me and let Moore and White put it on my bill. You are a great bunch of men. You are in the most useful profession there is. I know they don't pay you half the time, but to relieve a human being in suffering, that's the greatest epitaph that can appear on any man's tombstone."

Thus, *Ether and Me or "Just Relax"* becomes Volume 1, of Series I, of the Writings of Will Rogers. The other five books in this series are: *There's Not a Bathing Suit in Russia & Other Bare Facts; The Illiterate Digest; Letters of a Self-Made Diplomat to His President; Rogers-ISMS: The Cowboy Philosopher on the Peace Conference;* and *Rogers-ISMS: The Cowboy Philosopher on Prohibition.*

Since his death in 1935, there has been a continuing interest in Will Rogers. According to his niece, Mrs. Paula McSpadden Love, curator of the Will Rogers Memorial at Claremore, Oklahoma, "More than 15 million people have visited this popular shrine, and though the number who knew him personally is diminishing, the attendance increases each year. At present 75 per cent of the people who visit the memorial were not born at the time of Will Rogers' death, but he is known in each succeeding generation as evidenced by the references to him in papers, magazines and books. . . . We have calls and written requests from writers, politicians, news commentators, radio and TV producers, business men, advertising agencies and the average citizen who finds in Will Rogers that common sense philosophy and faith in our country that is needed today. I cannot emphasize adequately the importance of making the Will Rogers material available to the public."

A study designed to organize and publish the materials Will Rogers created has been undertaken by the Will Rogers Memorial Commission and Oklahoma State University to give back to the world, as completely as possible, the words, the wisdom and humility of this great American. Because of the nature of these materials, it was decided to reprint his books first, then his other writings, edited in accordance with the rigid standards recommended by scholarly organizations both in history and literature.

The Daily Telegrams of Will Rogers, about 3,000 pieces or nearly one-half million words, in a large measure put him at the pinnacle of his fame. These will be presented in three volumes in Series II of this project.

From 1920 through 1932, Rogers covered Presidential Nominating Conventions (Republican and Democratic) from which he sent some 40,000 words of "gags" or articles. These will be published as a single volume.

His weekly articles, nearly 700 in number, written between 1922 and 1935 on subjects as varied as Rogers' own curiosity and aggregating more than 800,000 words, will be organized into four volumes.

In addition, there are more than 500 Rogers' short articles entitled "The Worst Story I've Heard Today." Rogers credited each to a friend, who often was famous, sometimes obscure; typically Rogers added a thought-provoking and timely "moral." A single volume will be devoted to these stories.

More than sixty broadcasts which Rogers made between 1930 and 1935 for two sponsored radio programs possess a unity of their own for another volume.

Finally, a rich variety of other materials—advertisements, speeches, interviews, letters—will be presented in the most meaningful arrangement to assist the reader in understanding the development of Rogers' personality and the important role he played during the 1920's and 1930's.

We are indebted to many people for assistance in the preparation of this book. Will Rogers, Jr., Mary, and James, the surviving members of Rogers' immediate family, have preserved and deposited with the Will Rogers Memorial at Claremore personal papers and manuscripts so essential to the project. Will Rogers, Jr. provided an insightful preface for this first volume, and Mr. Robert W. Love and his wife, Paula McSpadden Love, as Manager and Curator of the Will Rogers Memorial, placed the entire collection of memorabilia and archival materials at our disposal and offered many valuable suggestions.

Others who have rendered significant services and continue to respond with enthusiastic cooperation include: The Will Rogers Memorial Commission and the Editorial Advisory Committee at Oklahoma State University, whose members are listed elsewhere in this column; President Robert B. Kamm of Oklahoma State University; Mr. E. Moses Frye, University Legal Counsel; Dr. Marvin T. Edmison, Director of the Research Foundation and Assistant Vice President for Academic Affairs; Dr. Robert D. Erwin, Director of the University Development Foundation; Dr. Roscoe Rouse, Director of the University Library and his staff; and former Memorial Commission members Argene Clanton, Earl Sneed and the late Morton R. Harrison. Our special thanks go to Mr. John Hamilton, Director of the Oklahoma State University Press, and Glenn D. Shirley, his assistant, who not only designed the book but also offered vital editorial help, and to others who made contributions too numerous to mention.

Finally, we are extremely grateful to the Kerr-McGee Foundation, Phillips Petroleum Corporation, Mr. and Mrs. Robert W. Love, and the Legislature of the State of Oklahoma for generous financial support.

Joseph A. Stout, Jr.
EDITOR

Preface by Will Rogers, Jr.

In this book, Will Rogers treats his gallstone operation as a laughing matter. It was no such thing. From the start, its seriousness was recognized. As complications developed, it became touch-and-go.

I remember when my mother brought the three of us children into her room. With tears in her eyes, she told us of the operation and the troubles which were developing. At her direction we all knelt and prayed for Daddy's life. We were not an especially religious family. To my knowledge, this is the only time we ever knelt and prayed together. The large sun-drenched room, mother's tears, her air of quiet desperation; it is one of my most vivid memories. We were living in the Beverly Hills house. Will Rogers called it, "The House that Jokes Built." It was on a low hill, rambling two-story, with a long veranda. We seldom came into our parents' bedroom. This made it all the more impressive. I was sixteen and the eldest. To me, my father was indestructible. As mother talked, suddenly the world began crumbling away. I remember feeling very grown up, very responsible. I would protect the family. Neither my sister, then fourteen; nor my brother, then twelve, remembers that scene in the morning bedroom before our visit to the hospital. But for me, it was my first realization of life and death. So, while I have to laugh in re-reading this story, it brings back some deep memories. I know the heart-breaking reality on which it is based.

We were a close family, and never more close than when we were living in this Beverly Hills home. Beverly Hills, at the time, was mostly empty blocks of streets with the land farmed as a bean field. Below our house we had a stable and a large oval riding ring. The family album is full of pictures of Dad and the kids riding around the ring together, swimming in the pool together, tap-dancing together.

Several years before his operation, soon after he first came west to make silent pictures, Will Rogers tried producing two-reel comedies on his own. They were not successful. He only made three. The third one was called, *One day in 365*. The idea was the difficulties of a man trying to make movies and keep his home life under control at the same time. In other words, it was the funny things in his own life.

In the movie, the producer (Will Rogers) was trying to concentrate on the script while the expensive crew waited for him all day on the studio set. Meanwhile the kids (we three, happily playing ourselves) were fighting with the neighbor kids, upsetting the horses, getting into the cake, etc. etc. It was a silent comedy and, of course, exaggerated (I am sure we were never *that bad*). But it was our family picture. It was made with warmth and love and based on real life.

I think that is a most important ingredient in Will Rogers' humor—reality. Unlike most humorists, he seldom told "tall tales" about how - the - roof-fell-in-when-cousin-Zeb-was-sparkin'-in-the-parlor-and -the - bull - climbed - in-the-second-story-window-when-the-fire-department-arrived. When Will Rogers tells a story like *Ether and Me,* the details may wander about a bit, but the basic events are as they actually occurred. He invented the gags, never the situation.

He was naturally witty. At the dining table we were often laughing at the things he said. At the time I thought that all fathers made jokes. It wasn't till many years later that I learned otherwise and how unusual he was. Many, in fact I would say most, of his brilliancies first came ad lib out of his conversation. I remember one large Sunday buffet at our Santa Monica Ranch. Dad and I were in polo clothes ready for the game which would take place in an hour or so at the Uplifters Club. He was with a group of men discussing the Japan-China situation. Someone said that after all, all Japan wanted was a Monroe Doctrine over China. "Doctrin'," Dad said quick as a flash, "That's not doctrin'. That's operatin'." I remember saying to myself, "I'll bet that goes in the column." Sure enough it appeared a few days later in "Will Rogers Says," the column of a few paragraphs that he wrote each day and was printed on the front page of nearly 400 morning newspapers across the country. Of course, in the column, the thought was re-worked to bring out the point and minimize the pun. On these matters Will Rogers was always a careful craftsman. But the thought had just sprung out of conversation; it was not the result of hard thinking over a typewriter.

Like good conversation, important events stimulated him. He was at his best when the news was at its sharpest. He often said that Sunday, for his Monday morning column, was the hardest day to write. The Sunday papers had little hard news. They were mostly filled with "The Week in Review" and long feature articles. His best remarks were on the most immediate and most felt issues—the depression, the farm crisis, war, peace, unemployment. "Been millions made in wheat last week, but not by anyone who ever raised any." "It wasn't that Calvin Coolidge didn't do nothin'. It was that he did it *better* than anyone else." He needed real people, real events. He was a humorous commentator and not, like Mark Twain, a humorous writer. Without the real event of his operation he probably never would have written of hospitals, nurses, doctors and medicine.

Will Rogers wrote all of his own material. For an active comedian constantly appearing before the public this was, and still is, almost unprecedented. Even in his day, performers had their stable of "gag-writers." Today, of course, they come in sets of five to a dozen. When a Hollywood gag man wrote, "Will, I'll write gags for you for a thousand dollars a week," Rogers replied, "For a thousand a week, I'll write gags for you." And he could have, too.

There was no malice to his humor. No hate. In the field of political humor this is very unusual. Most practitioners of the form develop into not just partisans, but violent, unforgiving partisans. Most commentators can be characterized as "left-wing comedians" or "right-wing comedians." Will Rogers was almost unique in that throughout his entire career he kept on an even keel.

Because his material was his own, his writings have a definite, underlying philosophical tone. The tolerant attitude, the skeptical doubt of perfection being achieved on this earth (especially by politicians), the friendly warmth; these come through even in his most cutting criticisms.

When divisions appeared in the country, he used his voice as a moderating influence. In the great depression, when this country was as angry, and the political rhetoric against the incumbent as mean as it had ever been, Will Rogers wrote, "Now listen, you people. Quit blaming President Hoover. And quit blaming the Republicans. Why, they're not smart enough to have thought of all the things that have been happening to us lately."

He was amazingly productive. In addition to his constantly changing theatrical act, his lecture tours and his major banquet appearances (for which he often would prepare notes for an entire speech geared for that one occasion), Will Rogers wrote a weekly newspaper column, his famous daily column, magazine articles and, though they were mostly from other material, six books. His collected works run over two million words. Even removing the inevitable repetitions, he was, from 1923-1935, one of the more prolific writers of his time.

It is hard, a half century later, to look back and appreciate what he meant to the country. In addition to being its most real columnist, he was the leading after dinner speaker, a personality that made national news wherever he went. In the years when motion pictures dominated the mass entertainment, his movies were always setting box office records.

In those days everyone knew the Will Rogers story. He was a household figure—the Oklahoma cowboy, part Indian, who became the world's greatest roper and later, in the Ziegfield Follies, the country's most popular comedian. Statistically, he was about as untypical as one could get, but he was always called the "typical American." He was the man equally at home with kings and taxi-drivers, presidents and farm-hands. People felt that should he appear in their living room, he would be just family. His writings reinforce this impression. To a large extent it was true. Unlike most humorists, Will Rogers liked people—personal and en masse. The man and his writings were one.

This is the first volume of the collected works of Will Rogers. It is a project on which Oklahoma State University has been working for many years. Not only the Rogers family, but all who have admired the man and his writings are deeply grateful to the University for this effort.

It is, in many ways, a unique effort. As far as I am aware, it is the first time that the writings of a humorous commentator will have been presented in their entirety and with the scholarly apparatus usually reserved for more documentary history. In the field of editorial scholarship, this project will be breaking many new grounds.

Over the years, under the guidance of Mrs. Paula Love, the curator, the Will Rogers Memorial at Claremore has gathered, cataloged and assembled Will Rogersana. But it is a single collection at a single place. Scholars, wanting to use Will Rogers on events of the twenties and thirties, must visit Claremore. In their own libraries they can find but little of use.

The Will Rogers Research Project will remedy that. It will enable future generations of Americans to look at a segment of their past through the eyes of a very witty, very perceptive, and very profound man.

As one who has been close to this project since its inception, my special thanks go to Dr. Robert B. Kamm, President, Oklahoma State University; Dr. Theodore L. Agnew, the project's first Director; Dr. Homer L. Knight, former Head of the Department of History; Dr. Odie B. Faulk, present Head of the Department of History; and Dr. Joseph A. Stout, Jr., Director of the Will Rogers Research Project and Editor of the present volume.

ETHER AND ME

I - 1

ETHER AND ME

Here's a fact that might interest you: This is a yarn about a suffering Actor.[1]

Now I knew a man that always subscribed for the Congressional Record. It, of course, mentioned the fact if any Member of Congress had passed away. So he said he always took it because he just loved to read about dead Congressmen. Oftentimes you have been made to suffer by Actors. So you will be tickled to death to read about an Actor who suffers, and the more continuous he suffers, the more you will like it.

Now Irvin Cobb[2]—bless his ugly old frontispiece—not only gave us many a laugh with his classical Operation Book but he showed us the practical side of humor by making an operation pay its way.[3]

'Course Cobb could do it on his, and maybe Bernard Shaw[4] might if the operation was only a shave. But if mine's not humorous, why, don't blame me.[5] It's hard to be funny when you know the check will only pass through your hands.

We kid about our Doctors and we hate to pay 'em after it's all over and we have quit hurting. But I expect a lot of us have got 'em to thank for being here. So I dedicate both check and book to two charming members of an ancient and —I hope—honorable craft—Drs. Percy G. White, and Clarence E. Moore.[6] Don't be misled by their effeminate given names. They are a couple of big rough bruisers, physically.

This story opens on the bank of the Verdigris River in the good old Indian Territory, four miles east of a town called Oo-lo-gah, and twelve miles north of a town called Claremore—best Radium water in the World.[7] The plot of the story is a pain in the stomach. The stomach was located amidships of a youth who was prowling up, down, in and across said Verdigris River.

The plot first appeared when the stomach was at a tender and growing age. It would generally appear after too many green apples, too many helpings of navy beans, of which said stomach has always been particularly fond, and right after hog-killing time. With the back-bones and cracklins and chit-lins, the old plot would bob up again.

As I think back on it, we were a primitive people in those days. There were only a mighty few known diseases. Gunshot wounds, broken legs, toothache, fits, and anything that hurt you from the lower end of your neck on down as far as your hips was known as bellyache. Appendicitis would have been considered as the name of a new dance or some new game with horseshoes. Gallstones would have struck us as something that the old-time Gauls would heave at the Philistines or the Medes and the Persians—maybe get up on Mount Mussolini and roll them down on 'em.

Nervous indigestion was another unknown quantity. In order to have it you had to be nervous and in order to be nervous you had to imagine you had some imaginary illness and that nobody understood you.

Well, in those days, when you felt that way and couldn't explain why you were queer, why, they had an asylum for you. There was no such thing as indigestion then, as everybody worked. Of course, when a bunch was talking and there was quite a sprinkling of girls and women, why, we did have such a parlor name for this plot as Cramp Colic; that was the Latin for bellyache.

I don't remember when I first had it, but I sure do remember one of my dear old Mother's remedies for it. They just built a fire in the old kitchen stove and heated one of the old round flat kitchen stove lids—the thing you take off the stove if you want what you're cooking to burn. Well, they would heat it up — not exactly red hot, but it would be a bright bay. They took it off, wrapped it up in something and delivered it to your stomach with a pair of tongs.

We didn't know what a hot-water bottle was, and the only thing made out of rubber then was boots and the top of lead pencils and gents' wearing collars. A drug store had to get their money then out of paregoric, Cheatam's Chilli Tonic[8]

and pills by subscription. There were no rubber goods, banana splits, steaks, lettuce sandwiches, flivvers and flasks. In those days a rolling pin was made to flatten out a pan of biscuits and not to flatten out the starches in a protruding stomach.

Well, the heat from one of those stove lids burned you so you soon forgot where you were hurting. It not only cured you but it branded you. You would walk stooped over for a week to keep your shirt from knocking the scab off the parched place. Anybody that would look at you who was not familiar with a stove cap would think that an elephant had stepped on you. All it needed was the little scalloping around the edges to make it look like where his toes had sunk in.

After a little spell of this the plot maybe wouldn't show up for a year or maybe two years. Well, a little thing like that didn't compose much sickness for a strong-bodied and weak-minded old boy to have. Having a cramp colic every two or three years didn't hardly bring me under the heading of what you would call a invalid.

Oh, yes, I did have some chills, too, one summer, from what we afterwards learned was malaria. I used to have one every other day. Some people have them every day, but you can't expect in this world to have everything. Days when there were no chills billed with me I could get out and do a fair Kid's day's work, but on chill days I didn't punch the clock at all. My day's work was to chill, and I hope I am not egotistical in saying it, but I did a good job at it. I had it down pat.

This is the way you chill: First you get cold and you shake, your teeth chatter and your body commences shimmying. It's the same thing Gilda Gray[9] got and never got over. Only she was smart to cash in on it. City folks call it a dance; we call it a disease. Then after the shaking is over you get a fever and your head hurts like it is going to bust. When the head quits hurting and the fever goes away, why, that's all there is to the chill; it's over—that is, it's over for that day.

I used to try to have them two days running so that would give me a few days off; but, no sir, you couldn't do it, those chills knew when they were going to happen and they happened. If you get chills that is working right, you can make a bet on when it is going to happen. A lot of people in those days who had chilling children didn't have to keep a clock

or a calendar. If Lizzie had a chill early in the week you'd know it was ten o'clock Monday morning. Quinine was a regular food, not a medicine. It set on the table the same as sugar. The minute you would take it you'd eat something right quick to take away the taste, but you never could do it quick enough.

Well, I finally shook the chills off and in years to come I never was bothered with them any more. But the old plot of the piece, the stomach ache, she would play a return date about every couple of years. I had it here in the movies one day when I was working, and they put a mustard plaster on it, as there was no such thing as a stove cap in Hollywood. They had all been replaced by the can opener. Well, with this plaster on my stomach, I unconsciously did the funniest scene I ever did in my life. It was in a picture called Jubilo.[10]

Well, to go on with the plot. It hadn't shown up in years, until one spring,[11] on my tour of national annoyances, I hit a

town called Bluefield, West Virginia. I hadn't been there long when the old plot showed up. Now ordinarily when a pain hits you in the stomach in Bluefield, West Virginia, you would take it for gunshot wounds. But the old town has quieted down now and the sharpshooters have all joined the Kiwanis and Rotary Clubs. So I knew it wasn't wounds. Then the pain struck me before the nightly lecture and I knew no one would shoot me before the lecture, unless by chance he had heard it over in another town.

Well, the next time it hit me was just a few weeks later, out at my old ranch on the Verdigris River, in the same house where I was born and where I had previously balanced those flat irons on my stomach years before. My niece, who was living there and had a baby, she gave me some asafetida. The only thing it tastes like is spoiled onions and overripe garlic mixed. And the longer after you have taken it, the worse it gets. If I was a baby and I found out that somebody had given me that, if it took me forty years to grow up, I would get them at the finish, even if it was my mother.

Just a few nights after that, and my last night on the train coming home to check up on the moral conditions of Beverly and Hollywood, the Sodom and Gomorrah of the West, that night the old pain hit me again. You see, the plot is slowly thickening. Instead of quitting me after a few hours as it generally had, it kept hanging on. If it did go away, it would be right back.

When I got home they called in a doctor. He gave me some powders. The pain just thrived on those powders. I never saw a pain pick up so quick as it did when the powder hit it. Instead of setting around like most people do, I would take a stool or chair and arrange myself over it something like this: My head and arms would be on the floor on one side and my knees and feet on the floor on the other side. My middle was draped over the seat of the chair.

Finally my wife called in Doctor White, a famous physician. He had assisted us in some other family illnesses and we knew his telephone number. Well, he came and he had one of those old-time phonograph tubes where you stick one end in each ear, hold the other up against your chest and see what you can get. The static must have been something terrible, because he pulled it away and shook his head. I thought maybe that he had found out that I wasn't breathing and didn't know it. Then he would lay his hand on my stomach and thump the back part of his own hand with his other one. That formed a kind of contact and gave him sort of a new connection—or a wave length.

7

"What part of your stomach hurts?" he asked.

"Practically all of it, Doc."

I almost forgot to tell you that the first part he got to thumping and feeling around on was down low on the right-hand side, where I had always been led to believe the appendix is. I says, "There's where you are wrong, Doc; that's

the only part that don't hurt." He says, "Are you sure there's no pain there?" "I'm absolutely sure, Doctor." Well, that seemed to kind of lick him. An appendicitis operation within his grasp, and here it was slipping through his hands. He looked kind of discouraged.

But he was a resourceful fellow. He never, like a lot of these other doctors, hung all his clothes on one line. I could see his mind was enumerating other diseases that were not down so low. He commenced moving his thumping and listening around to other parts. He began to take soundings around the upper end of the stomach. When I told him it hurt there, I never had any idea that I was announcing a lead for pay dirt. When I told him where the pain was worse, his face began to brighten up.

Then he turned and exclaimed with a practiced and well-subdued enthusiasm, "It's the Gall Bladder — just what I was afraid of." Now you all know what that word "afraid of," when spoken by a doctor, leads to. It leads to more calls.

Now I had heard of the gall bladder in a kind of indirect way, but I never had given much thought about where it was or what it was doing. He then said, "Look up." And as I looked up he examined the lower parts of my eyes. Then he says, "Yes, it's Gallstones." Then I says, "Doc, are they backed up as far as my eyes?" I asked him. "What do you do for them?"

He didn't answer me direct, but he casually inquired if I had had a good season. I told him that outside of Waxahachie, Texas, Hershey, Pennsylvania, Concord, New Hampshire, and Newton, Kansas, I had got by in paying quantities.

He then says, "We operate." My wife says, "Operate?" And as soon as I came to enough I says, "Operate?"

My wife says, "Is there no easier way out?"

Then I showed that the pain had not entirely dulled my intellect. "Yes, is there no cheaper way out? Can't they feed me something heavy to wear out the stones?"

"No," he says. "You will always be bothered. The best way is to go down and have them taken out. . . . Where's the phone?"

I didn't know whether he was going to phone for the knives, the hearse, the ambulance or what. The wife pointed to the phone kind of dumfounded. Why didn't I think of telling him the phone was not working? That would have stalled the thing off a little longer. Well, he phoned for what seemed like a friend, but who afterwards turned out to be an accomplice. These doctors nowadays run in pairs and bunches.

This is a day of specializing, especially with the doctors.

9

Say, for instance, there is something the matter with your right eye. You go to a doctor and he tells you, "I am sorry, but I am a left-eye doctor; I make a specialty of left eyes." Take the throat business for instance. A doctor that doctors on the upper part of your throat he doesn't even know where the lower part goes to. And the highest priced one of all of them is another bird that just tells you which doctor to go to. He can't cure even corns or open a boil himself. He is a Diagnostician, but he's nothing but a traffic cop, to direct ailing people.

The old fashioned doctor didn't pick out a big toe or a left ear to make a life's living on. He picked the whole human frame. No matter what end of you was wrong, he had to try

to cure you single-handed. Personally, I have always felt that the best doctor in the world is the Veterinarian. He can't ask his patients what is the matter—he's got to just know.

Well, after a while I heard a big expensive car coming up our driveway hill. It made it. After years of listening we can tell the calibre of our callers by how many times they have to shift gears on our hill inside the yard. When they make it on high without a shift, we go to the door. On a one-shift noise, we let the maids go—I mean the maid. And on a complete stall, why, everybody ducks and no one is at home. Well, this fellow came up on high and right on upstairs, and they met.

There was a kind of knowing look between them, as good as to say, "I think we can get him."

This new one was Dr. Clarence Moore, the operating end of the firm. He is the most famous machete wielder on the Western Coast. He asked the same line of questions, but before I could get a chance to answer them myself, why, Doc White answered them for me the way they should be answered, to show that I had a very severe case of Gallstones. Right away this guy asked about the pain down around that old appendix, but the other one answered him with rather a sigh, "No, it's not there; but I have discovered a better place for it."

It seems the appendix is always their first shot. The first doctor said, "What do you think?" The second one says, "I think Gallstones." The first one says, "That's what I said." I says, "I'm glad you boys are guessing together."

"What do you advise?" the first doctor asked. "I advise an operation," said the second. "That's what I advised," said the first.

Imagine asking a surgeon what he advises! It would be like asking Coolidge, "Do you advise economy?"[12]

My wife said, "When?" The whole thing seemed to have gone out of my hands. I was just lying there marked Exhibit A.

One doctor was for doing it that night, but the next one was more of a humanitarian. He suggested the next morning. Well, Number One rushed to the phone again and called up. I couldn't think who they would be calling now; they already had the doctor and the surgeon.

I says, "The only other man he can possibly work with is the undertaker." But I was relieved to hear that it was only the hospital he was calling. He was asking for a nice room. I heard him say, "Yes, we'll be there in the morning."

My wife says, "Doctor, is there any danger in this operation? Well, as bad as I felt, I had to laugh at that. They re-

plied together in unison: "Why, there is just about a half of one per cent," as though they had rehearsed it.

I thought, "Those babies have pulled that one many a time. Half of one per cent! That's the chance people have got of taking a drink in this country—is half of one per cent —and look what's happening!"

They are reaching for their hats and all smiling, and you would have thought we had all made a date to have some fun and go hear Aimee preach.[13] They said they would take me down to the hospital and see how I got along.

Well, after the doctors had left, that gave my wife and I a chance to do a little thinking. What they had talked about had scared the pains clear away. We got to wondering what had brought on this severe attack at this time. We laid it to everything we could think of. Will Hays[14] had just been out here and spent the day with us. Now I don't lay the illness directly on to him, but a continual listening to the merits of the Movies and the Republican Party will sometimes react disastrously on a previously ailing stomach.

My wife was setting on the edge of the bed and we were

talking it over. She got up and left, and I thought to myself: "Poor Betty, she can't stand this; it's too much for her; she's gone so I can't see her." I got up and went in to console her. She was digging in an old musty leather case marked Insurance Papers.

Well, the household was up bright and early next morning to get old Dad off to the hospital. The whole place was what the novelist would call agog. Even the chauffeur—part time—had the old car shined up. This going to a hospital was a new thing to me. I had never been in one in my life only to see somebody else. Outside of those stove-lid episodes, I had never even been sick a day in my life. I had been appearing on the stage for some twenty-odd years and had never missed a show.

But I was going to make up for it now. They were taking me to the Swedish Lutheran Hospital. I knew nothing about it myself. It didn't make much difference what denomination I was cut under, but the reason we went there was because Lindbergh was at his height then, and I felt like out of respect to him we ought to make it a Swedish year.[15]

We went right in. A hospital is the only place you can get into without having baggage or paying in advance. They don't hold the trunk like a hotel does—they just hold the body.

They had a pretty, cozy room for me. The whole thing was like a big hotel, and I thought I was in the wrong place, because I couldn't smell Iodoform. Everything was jolly and laughter. The stomach had quit hurting, of course. Did you ever have a tooth hurt after you got to the dentist? I couldn't see any use in going to bed at ten o'clock in the morning when I hadn't been out the night before.

Then in came the nurse. Wow! I got one look at her and made it continuous. They introduced her as Miss. She was Ziegfeld's front row without a dissenting vote.[16] I got one look at Mrs. Rogers, who was looking her over also, and then she says, "Doctor, is this operation necessary?" I spoke up ahead of the doctor and said, "I'm beginning to think it is." Then I thought to myself, if this girl is this good looking and still single, she has let all her patients die, for if one ever got out alive they would nailed onto her.

Oh, say, I like to forgot to tell you that during this time I was turning yellow. One of the symptoms of the gall is that it produces jaudice.

Well, the doctors were both remarking, "Very yellow—he is getting yellower." Ha-ha! They didn't know it, but I wanted to tell them that that yellow was from the heart and not from the liver and gall bladder. They gave instructions about what to do to get me ready for tomorrow. I didn't think I had anything to do only just furnish the stomach. Then I thought maybe the surgeon wanted to practice a little in the meantime.

ETHER AND ME

The hilarity was at its height. You'd have thought there was going to be a picnic at the hospital the next day. One thing got me—a great big old hundred-and-eighty-pound lummox having women fussing around him when it didn't seem like he needed them. But later on, I was mighty glad to have them doing something, I tell you. The night nurse was also a very pleasant, cheerful, fine, capable little woman.

Things were going fine now, around the hospital, but up around the old Rogers Igloo things were stirring. The night before the operation, Mrs. Rogers got to studying: "Now these two men just came in here and they say there should be an operation. Of course I know they are fine capable men, the best doctors to be secured on the Western Coast, but I just wish I could get some more advice."

Then she gets hold of Mary Pickford, who lives on the expensive end of the same hill and has a very widely seen house. Betty thinks Mary is mighty smart.[17] In fact, everybody that knows Mary has that same single-track thought. She knew Mary must have a pretty good doctor, for he had been able to keep Doug jumping all these years, and so she thought: "Maybe he can do something for *my* handsome Douglas."[18]

Mary's doctor was out of town. But she knew another one and told my wife about him. She got him. You see, Betty got to thinking, after all the shooting was over, and while I was down in the hospital waiting to be operated on: "Now there's old Will. While he hasn't been a good husband, he's done about the best he could and knew how. While he's been funny to some people he has, at times, been very sad to me. But as ornery as he is, I'm not going to give him up without a struggle."

You see, she had, during our years of association with stage and screen people, seen so many second husbands who hadn't even turned out to be as good as the first that it set her wondering. Then our old friend Bill Hart[19] called up. He had a fine Doctor that he wanted her to talk to and have see

15

me. So she asked our two if they minded her having these other two look me over and all confer.

Well, they of course didn't and they knew it would make her feel better to have more opinions on it, and they felt their case would stand up before any witnesses. She made them promise that they wouldn't operate the next morning until they had held this foursome over my fairway.

All the time they were going ahead getting me all ready. The night before they wrapped my stomach all up in a bandage. I guess that was so no doctor could get at it ahead of them. Then there was a battalion of blood experts.

Every few minutes there would be a girl come in dressed like a manicurist and carrying a manicure set. She would say, "Hold out your left hand." Well, I wouldn't know whether she was going to wash it, kiss it, hold it or read it. She would take a sharp knife and take the tip end of one finger and cut it and get the blood and put it in a cute little container. I would just get settled down to steady worrying again when in would pop another one. She wanted the same thing only a different finger.

Finally one came in after all the fingers had been tapped, and I said "Good joke on you, there aren't any left." But she kept right on a-coming and grabbed me by the ear, the same way we do when we are going to ear down a bronc to get a hackamore on him. She just slit the lower end of the heavy-set part of my ear. I told her my ear-marks used to be; To crop and split the right and underslope the left. I didn't tell her, though, that we also dewlapped 'em.

I says, "Is there some particular brand of blood that you get from the ear that perhaps wouldn't go in any other locality?" She smiled sweetly, rolled up my ear's blood in a tube and says, "Thank you."

Well, by then I was growing weak from loss of blood. It got so every time a girl would come along with a tray I would start holding out my hands or my ears. I was beginning to think that some of them were keeping a friend who might be anaemic.

The next morning, after what should have been breakfast—but I didn't get any, as they won't operate on a full stomach—in filed the battalion of doctors. Betty was with them. One says, "He is yellow." Then each of the others said, "Yes." One of the new ones would ask a question and before I had a chance to answer, why, one of my original cast would explain in so many fewer words than I could. They listened and they thumped the same as the first one did. They discussed it all between themselves. I, the defendant, wasn't put on the stand at all. Finally they filed out.

Imagine your life in the hands of a quartet! I'd rather

trust a tenor. I wanted to get a chance to instruct the jury, but nothing doing. The clinic was over. The nurse and I were alone. Betty had gone out too.

I says, "How long do you think the jury will be out, and do you think there is any chance of a disagreement?" A hung jury was the best I could hope for. I knew a verdict in my favor was out of the question. I could see by the way they acted that the doctoring profession was a kind of a closed corporation, and while they might be professional rivals, they wouldn't purposely do each other out of anything. I asked the nurse again how she thought things would turn out.

She said, "Oh, they have the operating room engaged; they will have to go through with it now."

"Well," I said, "I had better go ahead then, for I certainly don't want to cancel an operating room. Those people up there are going to be all broken up if I don't come up and be all cut up. But I wonder if there is not someone that would like a nice operation, and I could send them up in my place."

There was a knock on the door and the jury came in. It stood four for operation. In fact five, for poor Betty had been won over with tales of the advantages of a nice neat operation. I knew the minute they opened the door that I had lost, for they all came in a smiling and said, "You are going to feel fine when this is over."

I thought: "Yes, it depends on how I have lived, where I will finish when this is over."

Well, it is customary, I have heard, for the defendant to shake hands with the jury, but that's only in case he's acquitted. They all went out, but forgot to shut the door, and I heard my two bidding the other two goodbye, thanking them and saying, "We'll do as much for you sometime, boys."

My surgeon stepped back into the room with his Vassar graduating gown on. That shows you the verdict was framed beforehand, for they must have had those suits under their others. Oh, they were tickled to death. If they had been doctor golfers, you would have thought they had broken a hundred and ten. Well, I saw right away they were going to make me a hole-in-one.

The main carver said he had a lot of other operations on that day, but that mine would be first. I asked him if he couldn't take somebody else first — that there might be someone in pain and that I had never felt better in my life. Then I thought his hand might be a little shaky early in the morning.

They put on me a pair of what looked like flannel boots that came pretty nearly up to the knee. They looked like those goloshes that girls wear in the winter and don't fasten the buckles, and when they come down the street they sound like a mule that's running loose with chain harness on. I never did find out what those boots were on me for, unless it was to catch the blood in case I got up and ran out, or to keep me from biting my toe nails in case I got nervous during the operation.

I didn't have any kind of a shirt or nightgown on. I had a sheet kind of draped over me. All I needed was my hands crossed. They tied a white thing around my head. Then all I needed was a Klan card. The doctor had a thing over his mouth so he wouldn't catch the same disease I had.

Bill Hart, bless his old heart, was there. He, like all good sportsmen, wanted to be in at the death. I was on the wagon and all ready. We were waiting signals from the operating room. Betty, God bless her, came over to hold my hand. I told her to go over and hold the surgeon's hand for the next thirty minutes and we would all be safe.

Then we got the signal that we were next. You never saw such hustling around. They seemed to think: "Do you realize there's not a soul in this place being whittled on at this minute?" I bid goodbye to my Betty and the parade started down the hall to the elevator. We passed another wagon with an old boy on it that had just come down. I wondered how he had made it. Then I heard him cussing, and I thought: "He's all right, and even if he passes out, he will have the satisfaction of telling them what he thought of them before he left."

As I was a-rolling to the operating room with my retinue

of nurses and doctors as outriders, I thought I ought to pull some kind of a gag when I got in there that would get a laugh. I had never seen one before. The only experience our family had had with operating rooms was when we had the children's tonsils and adenoids removed, which is a juvenile social re quirement in Beverly Hills.

There was a kind of a little balcony up above the operating-room floor where people with a well-developed sense of humor could sit and see other people cut up. It must be loads of fun. But there wasn't a soul in there for my operation. I felt kind of disappointed.

I thought, "Well, here I am maybe playing my last act and it to an empty house."

There were a lot of doctors and more nurses than I ever saw in my life. One nurse was there they told me afterwards just to count every single thing used inside you during the opening. Every gauze pack and every scissors and knife, no matter how small, has to be checked up and accounted for before any sewing up starts. This removes most of the old-time humor from operations, by making it impossible for anyone to joke about what was left inside them.

One fellow had a kind of a hose with a big nozzle on the end of it. Well, I had by this time thought of my joke and was all ready to pull it and set the whole place in a good natured uproar. I just opened my mouth to utter my comical wheeze when this old hose boy just gently slipped that nozzle right over my mouth and nose both. I wanted to tell him, "Just a minute!" And I started to reach up and snatch it off, and a couple of men who had enlisted as internes, but who in reality were wrestlers on vacation, had me by each hand. I certainly was sore. Here I had this last aspiring wise crack and it had been snuffed out before I could give vent to it. And what made it so bad, I can't think to this day what it was. I remember at the time I thought it was going to be a knock-out, but the gas and the ether completely knocked it into another world.

You see the first thing they bump you off with is gas; that puts you where you won't tell any bum gags. Then they give you the ether; that's the postgraduate course in knock-out drops. When you get that you don't even leave a call.

I knew this old boy was bothering me, but there was nothing I could do about it. After he had kept on a-smothering for a little bit it seemed like another fellow started hammering and drilling a hole through the side of the hospital and kept right on pounding and drilling right towards my head.

Then the birds started singing, but they only sang a minute, when we had a shipwreck and everybody on the boat was going down, and it looked like they were trying to push me under. Then there was a hall full of the craziest looking people. They would read off some numbers for one man and

then some for another, and then say, "There wasn't enough to nominate." And this same thing went on and on. They were just about to agree, when the world came to an end.

Then a farmer started running and hollering for relief, when somebody shot him to put him out of his mortgages. Another little fellow was a-running and hollering, "I don't choose to run." And all this time I was running faster than anybody. Then I was in a bus trying to make a grade crossing and the bus was crowded with people, and as you know, the trains never run fast until they get near a grade crossing, and they never hit a bus unless it's full.

Well, the train was right on us when the Chinese started shelling the town and saying, "We are Missionaries come to America, and you will have to worship Buddha and go to the Mission schools and learn Chinese." Then the Nicaraguans started dropping airplane bombs on us. We had nothing to do but let them drop. They said, "They wanted to protect the United States, as they wanted to put a canal through here some time."[20]

Then I was rehearsing with the Follies. Coolidge and I were working together. We had an act framed up where we had asked an Englishman to disarm and he started laughing and we couldn't get him stopped, and we had to ring down the curtain.

Then the water kept rising till it got up around the bed and there were women and children and horses and mules and levees and cotton gins and airplanes and boats, and a fellow got up in a big hall in a big city and said, "We can't pass this bill; it will take too much money. If it's passed, the income tax can't be lowered."[21]

Then another crevasse broke and we were drowning, when I heard the nurse on one side and my wife on the other both saying, "Lay perfectly still, you're all right. You are fine now. Just relax."

ETHER AND ME

How was I going to do anything else? Wasn't every bone in my body broke? Wasn't my throat cut? Couldn't I remember falling off a thirty-story building?

"You'll be all right. Just relax and go back to sleep. Yes dear, it's all over and you are fine," said my Betty.

"What's fine? I don't see anything fine. Didn't the airship burn up and me right in it?"

"The doctors are right here, dear."

"My Lord, have I got a retake? If this is what they call saving anybody, what did they save me for?"

"It's the ether."

"No, it's not the ether; it's me. I know what I'm doing—I'm dying, and you-all are just standing there while I do it. Damn the whole gang of you."

Finally this ether got to leaving me and I sort of remembered what the operation had been for. I asked them, "Did you get any gallstones?" I was interested in the quality and the karats. I thought they might find something unusual, for any stone that hurt me that bad must have had corners on it. I figured it must be a rough diamond.

Yes, they had got some, a couple of sizable dimensions, but nothing in any way approaching what could be used for exhibition purposes. I felt right then that the operation had been a failure. What's the use of having one if you couldn't show something worth crowing about?

I then asked, "Did you take out the Gall Bladder?" He had told me that he might jar me loose from that particular organ.

"No," they said. "We found a condition there that was unusual and it warranted us not taking it out at this time. But we found it, and if at any time you ever have any more trouble with it, why, it will be no trouble to go in and get it."

"Oh," I says, "you found out where it was?" This operation was in the nature of exploration or research. Well, I'm glad you located it, anyhow; but suppose in my jumping around over the country the way I do, trying to find a Democrat, what if this thing should change its location? It's liable to be here today and gone tomorrow."

I would keep seeing the doctors and nurses coming in and looking down on the floor at the side of my bed. I thought at first it was a dog under the bed. They would frown and look worried and then move away.

I says, "What's under there that's causing all these mysterious peeps?" The nurse said, "That's the drain from the tubes."

"Drain from what tubes?"

"Why, the tubes that the doctors put in your side."

"Why, I thought they opened me up to take out things not to put more in. You talk like there might be a series in there. How many are there, if it's a fair question?"

She looked and counted them and said, "Two."

Two? I was hoping there was more than that. You can never get much distance on one of those two tube sets. We had one at home in Beverly and all we could get would be: "Praise the Lord, make it a good collection. God loveth a cheerful giver." It was a woman's voice. I thought: "My goodness, I'm nothing but an old casing with a couple of inner tubes in me."

Well, all this worry of the doctor's was from the fact that I wasn't draining. They had found a rather unusual condition in there. Being in California, it would be unusual. I didn't have sense enough to know it, but I was in pretty bad shape, for this drain was over two days and nights showing up. It seems it wasn't due to defective plumbing, but there was sort of a stoppage in the main duct that comes down out of the liver.

Well, the doctors slept right there at the hospital. They were trying everything from glucose to Murphy's Drip. As bad as I felt, I could tell that something wasn't breaking just right. Things were looking bad for Claremore, Oklahoma's, favorite light-headed comedian. If things didn't show up pretty soon, it looked like I had annoyed my last President. Betty was a better actor than the doctors.

Finally it showed up. Doctor Moore got one look and shouted, "If I was a drinking man I would try some of my own prescriptions tonight." He was so tickled that I believe if I had paid my bill then I would have got fifty per cent off.

He tells me what shape I have been in and he sits down and takes a card out of his pocket and draws a blue print of the whole thing. That's one thing any Californian can do is draw a blue print showing you where in six months there'll be three banks, a subway and a department store right next to the lot he is trying to sell you.

The main duct—Now I'm going to get into some technical stuff here and it's only people that have had the advantages of superior operations will understand, so the riffraff better skip over this part; it's only for the Intelligentsia. You know there is nothing broadens one like an operation, both mentally and physically. You see, I spoke of duct. Now to you ordinary boneheads, duct is the thing a batter does when a pitcher throws one too close to his bean.

Well, here is what he drew as well as I can remember: There is a right lobe and a left lobe of the liver. A good deal depends on which side the trouble is on. If you eat more on the right side of the mouth, why, the trouble is likely to be in the right lobe, and vice versa. The map started in with the liver, so that was the North boundary by my trouble. What laid North or beyond that I have no idea; it may be the thorax or the medulla oblongata.

You know, the liver is shaped kind of like a boxing glove, and where it's laced up is where the big duct starts in. Just below it and sort of around the corner is what the oil men would call an offset. Near the termination of the wishbone, is a small sort of a pocket, or receptacle. This receptacle is not very large and you would hardly notice it if it didn't get stones crossways in its main entrance. It's called the gall gladder and

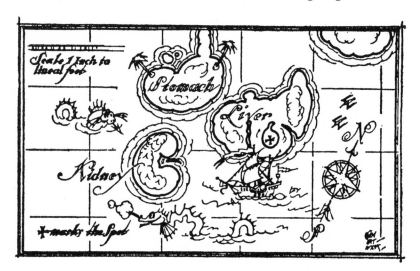

is shaped kind of like a hot dog that's been stuffed more at one end than the other.

Well, this main duct that runs from the liver South into the stomach runs by this little hot-dog stand, and there is a detour line that taps into this miniature gravel pit. Now it's this little alley that gets clogged up. Of course he had dug it out, but the main duct line above it was the one that wasn't running. No stone would be up there, for a stone won't float uphill.

Well, he explained it so easy I was sorry I hadn't taken up doctoring, for it looked mighty simple. He left me the map. He had written it on the back of a golf score, so I don't know now whether he went from the liver to the main duct in par, or if he took three's on the green. I could tell from the drawings that he was in the rough when he hit the little duct. The drawings looked like he had taken about three niblicks and two putter-mashies to get on the fairway down into the stomach.

Then I would get the nurse to draw what she thought had happened. 'Course she would have the liver on the opposite side and maybe shaped like a bonnet. But I just thought: "If everybody was shaped as different on the inside as they are on the outside, how does a doctor know what part of the body an organ would be located in?"

Take a long tall fellow; his interior furnishings must all be draped up and down, while with a little dumpy, short bird they must lay horizontal. For instance, they must operate on fat people with a sword instead of a knife, and on extremely slender people with a safety razor to keep from going clear through. Take, for instance, the changing waistline of the last few years. Suppose a doctor wanted to reach something directly under a line with it, he wouldn't know whether to lance the lady's shoulder or hip.

Then I had the nurse go to the hospital library and get the doctor books, and we would look at pictures of views taken in this locality, with X marking spot where stones were last seen. These books always showed the interior in colored photography; it looked almost like a Cecil de Mille movie.[22]

Now the Gall goes into this little pocket and remains until needed—that is, until you get sore at somebody and want to use it up on them. That's why it is that good natured people are the ones that have the Gall operations; they never get a chance to use it up on anybody.

Another thing I learned was that the complaint is more common by far among women than among men. Well, that fact didn't please me so much, as I was just bordering on the effeminate as it was. I also learned that it was more prevalent among Jewish people; that's what I get for going to those Kosher restaurants with Eddie Cantor.[23]

ETHER AND ME

Now, as I have so thoroughly and comprehensively explained the location of this, now what causes the stones to form? Well, there are various reasons. Republicans staying in power too long will increase the epidemic; seeing the same ending to Moving Pictures is a prime cause; a wife driving from the rear seat will cause Gastric juices to form an acid, and that slowly jells into a stone as she keeps hollering.

Of course I will always believe that mine was caused by no sanitary drinking cups in the old Indian Territory where I was born. We used a gourd, raised from a gourd vine. Not only did we all drink out of the same gourd but the one gourd lasted for years, till Prohibition weaned some of them away from water.

Then another thing I have thought of recently that might have caused it, which is that our handkerchiefs, when we bought them from the store, were not wrapped in sealed packages. They were just handled in the bulk. Some clerk might have had Gall trouble and slipped it to me in that way. I believe that if modern sanitary methods like the above hadn't come in when they did, that by now four out of five would have had gallstones.

But while lying in the hospital recuperating I just accidentally stumbled on what I really think caused the operation. For years I had carried a very big—that is, big for my circumstances—Accident and Sickness Disability Insurance. Well, I would notice that my wife would get a little irritable every year when it would come time to pay the premiums on these various sick and accident policies, and say, "Well, that's pretty large to carry, isn't it, when you never have got a cent out of it?" And I would admit it did seem like a bad investment.

It was getting terribly discouraging to keep paying year after year and not being able to get sick, and with no prospects of ever getting sick. Here I was betting a lot of insurance companies that I would get sick or hurt and they were betting me I wouldn't. Now if you think you are not a sucker in a case like that, all you have to do is to look at the financial standing of the company in comparison to the financial standing of the people who bet on the other side. It's just a case of somebody knowing more about you than you know about yourself.

Why, they have the highest priced doctors to look you over. If you look like nothing but lightning can kill you, why, he sends in a report to the company to go ahead and bet you that you won't get sick. But if you look the least bit like you are going to get sick, they don't bet you. Any time they approve of you, that should show you right there that there is nothing going to happen to you. But you, like a fool, go ahead and bet them in the face of all this professional knowledge that you know more than they do.

I argued with my wife, saying, "Well, I may get sick."

"Yes, you might get sick, but you never do."

Well, you see she had me licked. I then said, "I may get hurt in a polo game by falling off my horse."

She said, "No, you have fallen off so much, you've got used to it, so I have no more hopes along that line."

So last summer when paying time came, and as she's the banker, my insurance man—he really shouldn't be one, he's so different from the others—advised her to reduce the policies. They decided to cut down on the accident and disability, but they allowed the straight life to remain. They figured I would die, but that I would die without illness. Well, I didn't know the thing had been cut down.

One day I was a-laying in the hospital and I just happened to have the only bright thought that had come to me in weeks. "Say, this thing I'm doubled up here with comes under the heading of 'sickness'; it even comes under the heading of 'accident.' " For wasn't I getting well from an operation?

ETHER AND ME

So I thought of those policies I had been paying on for years. This sickness is going to turn out all right, at that. I began to think how I could stretch it out into what might be termed a slow convalescense. So I was grinning like a moving-picture producer who has just thought of a suggestive title to his new picture. So when my wife called again I broke the good news to her.

I says, "If we can get a bona-fide doctor to say that I have been sick and couldn't spin a rope and talk about Coolidge, we are in for some disability."

Well, I noticed the wife didn't seem so boisterous about this idea. Then I got to thinking: "Maybe I haven't been sick enough, or maybe I haven't got a bona-fide doctor."

Then the truth did slowly out; she told me the sad story of the cutting down of the insurance. It read like a sentence to me. She said my physical condition had misled them. Of course she said there would be some salvage out of our short-sightedness, but that the operation would be by no means money-making. Whereas if the original policies had prevailed I would have reaped a neat benefit.

So if you want to stay well, just bet a lot of rich companies that you will get sick; then if you can't have any luck getting sick, have the policy cut down, and before six months you'll be saying "Doctor, the pain is right there."

Of course I got this consolation: If I had had the bigger policy, why, it would have had some clause in there where I got sick on the wrong day or had the wrong disease or that policy didn't cover rock quarries. There would have been an alibi somewhere, for those four pages of clauses in a policy are not put in there just to make it longer.

So I guess everything happened for the best. After all, it's not the operation that's bad; it's the caster oil afterwards. I know now how Mussolini conquered Italy.[24]

Now I think anybody that suffers must do so with a view

30

or purpose in mind, and that's why I want to point a moral in this yarn.[25] When people have tonsils removed, they come out bragging about it and tell what the operation was for; the same with adenoids; and they start talking about their appendices before their wraps are off. But with Gall Bladder they never bring the name of the operation into public ear-shot. They say they have been operated on, but they don't say what for.

Now I figures out that it's the name that's against it. Now I don't know why that name should be a more offensive thing to speak of while the company is just settling down to steady scandal gossip than any other part of the body. It's just among a lot of other what the doctors call organs, and to operate on these with undesirable names should be no disgrace for conversational purposes. But it's just human nature; we always like something with some big name that we don't know anything about; some doctor for no reason at all, outside of the fee, called it the appendix. It had a nice sounding name. Now, everybody that don't know what to be operated on for, have their appendices removed.

Now the Gall Bladder means something; it's a real name of a real functioning organ, same as the heart functions—in some people. But the name is all wrong for living and dining room gossip. It's too crude, it's too sudden, it's not euphonius, it means too much what it is; it's like a toothpick—we want to use it but we don't want to let anybody know it. And as for operations, why appendices can't compare with this other.

Why, appendices are taken out just while they are looking for something else, while this other calls for a table, a lot of nurses and a bunch of ether; it's a surgeons' operation; while appendices is a hospital night-watchman's job. If we ever make it amount to anything as a topic, we have got to change its name, and I have been giving the name a lot of thought. I thought we ought to call it something from the Latin.

The word "Gaul" itself is not bad. Gaul was a nation that flourished when the flourishing was good, and was extinguished when the extinguishing was good. So it's the second word of the disease that makes the name objectionable. So what you say we take the first letter of the first name, which is G, and the first letter of the second name, which is B, and for euphonious reasons we add double E to each one of these and tack on an S to the last one for good measure and that gives us the word Gee-Bee's?

Now don't get this confused with Hee-BeeJeeBee's. What we've got or just had are just GeeBee's. Now that name means so little that it ought to become popular. It sounds good and has no objectionable features that I can see, and ought to give us entree anywhere. I don't want to just stand around a party and point to my scar and not be able to tell what disease put it there. This appendix crowd has lorded it over other operations long enough. Now that we've got a name with no harsh sounding words, let us GeeBee people step in and get some of the credit. Why, on account of its locations we can point with much more modesty to our scars.

But I am broad-minded. I think that all operations should be on an equality. Any time you have whiffed the ether, that should make you eligible to speak publicly and call your operation by its name, no matter what region is remodeled. If you have been overhauled, you should be eligible to enter any conversation, for you are then one of the Fraternity of Scarbellies.

So if I can lift the GeeBee's operation to the social standing in conversational circles that Appendix now occupies, then my illness will not have been in vain. Are you with me, GeeBee's? Then Scars front! Forward, march! Viva, Gee-Bee's!

THE END

SCARBELLY

by Will Rogers

(Original Manuscript)

This is a Serial in two parts, You may be one that dont like continued
stories, But this fact might interest you, its about a suffering Actor.
Now I knew a man that always subscribed for the Congressional Record,
It of course related the fact if any Congressman had died, So he said he
always took it because he just loved to read about dead Congressmen.
Now offtimes you have been made to suffer by Actors, So you will be
tickled to death to read about an Actor who suffers, and the more contin-
ous he suffers the better.

Now Irvin Cobb, (bless his old ugly frontispiece) not only gave us
many a laugh but he showed us the practical side of humor by making an
operation pay its way.

Now I tried to crowd all this misery into one Article and was having a
hard time doing it, Then the bill for the operation come, So I decided to
make it in two parts, You cant pay for a modern,up to date, with all
conveniences, operation with one Article, I dont care how high priced you
are you cant do it, Bernard Shaw couldent do it, even if he amputated his
whiskers, Operations have increased since Irv' had his, So if this is not
humorous why remember its hard to be funny when you know the check will
merely pass through your hands, Paying for an operation when you dont hurt
is like I imagine paying alimony would be.

This story opeans on the bank of the Verdigris river, in the good old
Indian Territory, four miles east of a town called Oo-la-gah, and 12
miles north of a city called Claremore, The plot of the stry is a pain in
the stomach, the stomach was located amidships of a youth who was prowling
up, down, in , and across, said Verdigris River, The plot first appeared
when the stomach was at a tender and growing age, It would generally appear
after too many green applaes, too many helpings of navy beans, of which
said stomach has always been particularly fond of, AND right after hog killing

35

times, with the backbones, and the cracklins, and the Chitlins, the old plot
would bob up again. As I think back on it, we was a primative people in those
days, There was only a mighty few known diseases, Gunshot wound, broken leg,
tooth ache, fits, and anything that hurt you from the lower end of your
neck on down as far as your hips, was known as "Bellyache", Apendicitis,
would have been considered as the name of a new dance, or some new game with
                            HAVE
horsehoes, Gall Stones would struck us as something that the old time Gauls
would   and
heave at the Phillistines the Meads and the Persians, Maby get up
                                                                OTHER
on Mount Mussolini and roll em down on em. Nervous Indijestion was an unknown
quantity, In order to have it you had to be nervous and in order to be nervous
          to   you had
you had/imagine/some imaginary illness, and nobody understtod you. Well in
those days when you felt that way and couldent explain why you were queer,
why they had an asylum for you. There was no such thing as indijestion then
as everybody worked. Course when a bunch was a talking and there was quite
a sprinkling of girls and women, why we did have such a parlor name for this
plot as Cramp Colic, that was the Latin for Bellyache, I dont remember when
                                      my dear old mothers
I first had it but I sure do remember one of/the remedies, They just built a
fire in the old kitchen stove and they heated one of the old round flat
kitchen stove lids, (the thing you take off the stove if you want your stuff
too burn) Well they would heat it up to about 90 degrees farenheighth, not
exactly red hot, but it would be a bright bay, They took it off wrapped it
up in something and delivered it to your stomack with a pair of tongs,
We dident know what a Hot water bottle was, the only thing made out of
                B
rubber then was a boots and the top for led pencils, and gents wearing collars,
A drug store had to get their money then out of Paregoric, Cheatams Chill toni
and pills, by subscription, There was no rubber goods, Banana splits, steaks,
Lettuce sandwiches, and flasks, in those days a rooling pin was made to
fllatten out a pan of biscuits, and not sold to flatten the starches in a
protruding stomach.

well the heat from one of those flat irons burned you so you soon forgot
where you was a hurting. It not only cured you but it braned you, you
would walk stooped over for a week to keep your shirt from knocking the scab
off the parched place, Anybody that wasent familiar with a stove cap, that
would look at your stomach would think that an elephant had
stepped on you, all it needed was the little scalloping around the edges
to make it look like where his toes had sunk in.

Well after a little spell of this it maby wouldent show up for a year or
maby two yeras, Well a lit le thing like that dident compose much sickness
for a strong bodied, weak minded old boy to have, Having a cramp colic
every two or three years, dident hardly bring me under the heading of what
you would call an invalid.

Oh yes I did have some chills, one summer. Too From what we afterwards learned
was malaria. I used to have one every other day. Some pople had t hem
every day but you can't expect in this world to have everything. Days
when there were no chills billed with me I could get out and do a fair
Kid's days work, but on chill days I didn't punch the clock at zll.
My days work was to chill and I hope I am not egotistical in saying it
but I did a good job at it, I had it down pat. This is the way you chill:
First you get cold and you shake, your teeth chatter, and your body commenced shimmying. It's the same thing Gilda Gray got and never got over.
Only she was smart enought to cash in on it. City folks call it a dance,
we call it a disease. Then after the shaking is over you get a
fever and your head hurts like it is going to bust. When the head
quits hurting and the fever goes away why thats all there is to the
CHILL, it's over, that is it is over for that day. I used to try to
have them two days running so that would give me a fewdays off, but no
Sir you couldn't do it, those chills knew when they were going to happen,
and they happened. If you get a chill that is working right all during

the summer, you can make a bet on when it is going to happen. A lot
of people in those days had two or three ~~good~~ chilling children didn't
who   *GOOD*
have to keep a clock or a calender. If Lizzie had a chill early in
the week you'd know it by ten oclock Monday morning. Quinine was a
regular food not a medicine. It set on the table the same as a sugar
bowl. The minute you would take it you'd eat something right quick
to take away the taste, but you never could do it quick enough.
Well I finally shook the chills off and in years to come I never was
bothered with them any more, but the old plot of the piece, the stomach
ache, she would play a return date about every ouple of years. I had
                                               c
her in the movies one day when I was working and they p ut a mustard
plaster on it as there was no such thing as a stove cap in Holloywood.
They had been replaced by the can opener. Well, with this plaster on
my stomach I unconsciously did the funniest scene I ever did in my
life/ It was in a picture called Jubilo ". ~~Years, during that~~ she
                                       TILL
hadn't shown up in years, till this Spring on my tour of National
                          l
annoyances, I hit a town called Bluefied, West Virginia. I hadn't
been there long when the old plot showed up. Now ordinarily when a
pain hits you in the s tomach in Bluefield West Virginia you would take
it for gunshot wounds, but the old town has quieted down now and the
sharpshooters have all joined the Lions and the Rotary Clubs. So I
knew it wasn't wounds. Then the pain struck me before the nightly
lecture and I knew no one would shoot me before the lecture, unless
by chance they had heard it over in another town. Well, the next time
she hit me was just a few weeks later out at my old ranch on the Verdi-
                                                        PREVIOUSLY
gris River in the same house where I was born and where I had balanced
these flat irons on my stomach years before. My niece who was living   *(ES*
there and had a baby, she gave me some asafoetida, the only thing it *TAST-*
like is spoiled onions and over ripe garlick mixed. And the longer

after you have taken it the worse it gets. If I was a baby and I found

out that somebody had give me that, if it took me forty years to grow

up, I would get them at the finish even if it was my mother. ~~XXXXXXXX~~

~~XXXXXXXXXXXXXXXXXXXXXXX~~ Just a few nights after that, and my

last night on the train coming ~~XXXXXXXXXXXXXX~~ *HOME* to check up on

the moral conditions of Beverly and Hollywood, the Sodom and Gomorrah

of the West. Well, that night the old pain hit me again. You see the

plot ^{is} slowly thickening. Instead of quitting me after a few hours as

she generally had, she kept a hanging on. If she did go away, she'd

be right back. They called in one Doctor. He gave me some powders.

Well that pain just thrived on those powders. I never saw a pain pick

up so quick as it did when powder hit it. Instead of setting round

like most people do, I would take a stool or chair ~~XXXXXXXXXXXXXX~~ *and arrange myself*

over it something like this: My head and arms would be on the floor
on one side, and my knees and feet on the floor on the other side.

My middle was draped over the seat of the chair. Well, finally my wife

called in Doctor White. He had assisted us in some other family illness-

es and we knew his telephone number. Well, he came, and he had one of

those old time phonograph tubes where you stick one end in each ear,

hold the other up against your chest and see what you can get. The

static must have been something terrible because he pulled it away

shaking his head. I thought maybe he had found out that I wasn't

breathing and didn't know it. Then he would lay his hand on my

stomach and thump the back part of his own hand with his other one.

That formed a kind of a contact and gave him sort of a new connection,

~~XXXX~~ a wave length. "What part of your stomach hurts"? he asked.

"Practically all of it, Doc". I likeed to forgot to tell you the first

part he got to thumping and feeling around on was down low on the right

hand side where I had always been led to believe these appendics are.

I says"there's where you are wrong Doc, that's the only part that don't

hurt". He says, "Are you sure there's no pain there?" "I'm absolutely
sure, Doctor.". Well, that seemed to kind of lick him. An appendics
operation within his grasp and here it was slipping thru his hands. He
looked kind of discouraged. But he was a resourceful fellow, He never,
like a lot of these other doctors, hung all his clothes on one line.

I could see his ~~####~~ mind was enumerating other diseases that were not
down so low. He commenced hoving his thumping and listening around to
other parts. He begins to take soundings around the upper end of the
stomach. When I told him it hurt there, I never had any idea that it
was announcing a lead for pay dirt. As I ~~announced~~ *SAID* where the pain was
worse his face began to brighten up. Then he turned and ~~announced~~ *EXCLAIMED* with
a practiced and well subdued enthusiasm,"It's the Gall Bladder. Just
what I was afraid of". Now you all know what that word "afraid of",
when spoken by a doctor, leads to. It leads to more calls. Now I had
heard of the Gall Bladder in kind of an indirect way, but I had never
given much thought about where it was or what it was doing. He then
said, "Look up", and as I looked up he examined the lower parts of my
eyes. Then he says, "Yes, it's Gall Stones". Then I says, "How can
you tell, Doc, are they backed up as far as my eyes"? I then asked him,
What do you do for them, ~~use them up~~"? (I ~~thought maybe~~ "*Can't*" they ~~could~~ feed
you something heavier ~~and~~ *to* wear out the stones. He says, "*Then*, we operate."
My wife says, "Operate"? and as soon as I came to enough I says,
"Operate"? My wife says, "is there no easier way out"? Then I showed
the pain had not entirely dulled my intellect. "Yes, is there no cheaper
way out"? He says, "No, you will always be bothered. The best way is
to go down and have them taken out. Where's the phone"? I didn't know
whether he was going to phone for the knives, the hearse, the ambulance,
or what. Lord what a fast worker this baby was. The wife pointed to
the phone kind of dumfounded. Why didn't I think of telling him t e
phone was not working. That would have ~~####~~ stalled the thing off a

little longer. Well, he phoned for what seemed like a friend, but who
afterwards turned out to be an accomplice. These Doctors ▓▓▓ nowadays
run in pairs or bunches. Well, after awhile I heard a big expensive car
coming up our driveway hill. It made it. After years of experience in
listening we can tell the calibre of our callers by how many times they
have to shift gears on our hill inside the yeard. When they make it on
high without a shift we go to the door. On a one shift noise , we let
the maids go(I mean the maid). And on a ▓▓▓▓▓▓▓▓ complete stall
why everybody ducks and nobody is at home. Well, this fellow came up
on high and right on up stairs, ▓▓▓▓▓▓▓ And they met. There was a
kind of a knowing look between them, as good as to say, "I think we can
get him". This was Doctor Clarence Moore, the operating end of the firm.
He is the most famouse"machete"wielder on the Western Coast. He asked
the same line of questions, but before I could get a chance to answer them
myself, why, Doc White answered them for me the way they should be ans°wered
to show that I had a very sever case of Gall Stones. Right away this Guy
asked about the pain down around that old appendics, but the other answered
him with rather a sigh, "No, it's not there, but I have discovered a
better place for it". It seems the appendics is always their first shot.
The first Doctor said, "What do you think"? The second one says, "I think
Gall Stones". The first one says, "That what I said". I says, "I'm
glad you boys are getting together". "What do you ▓▓▓▓▓", the first
advise?
Doctor asked. "I advise an operation", said the second. "That's what
I advised", said the first. Now can you imagine asking an ▓▓▓▓▓▓▓
▓▓▓▓▓ surgeon "what they advise"? It would be like asking Coolidge
"do you advise economy"? My wife said "When". The whole thing seemed
to have gone out of my hands. I was just laying there marked exhibit
A. One doctor was for doing it that night, but the next one was more of
a humanitarian. He suggested the next morning. Well, number one rushed

(Insert in page 7)

This is a day of specializing, especially with the Doctors. Say for
instance there is something the matter with your right eye. You go to
a doctor and he tells you"I am sorry but I am a left eye doctor, I
make a specialty of left eyes". Take the throat business for instance.
A doctor that doctors on the upper part of your throat he don't even
know where the lower part goes to. And the highest priced one of all
of them is another Bird that just tells you which one to go to. He
can't cure corns or open a boil himself. He calls himself a Diagnostician, but he's nothing but a traffic cop to direct ailing people.
The old fashioned doctor he didn't pick out a big toe or an left ear and to
make a life's living on. He picked the whole human frame. No matter
what end of you was wrong he had to try to cure you single handed.
                                                                is
Personally I have always felt that the best doctor in the world was a
                              his patients
Veterinarian. He can't ask what is the matter, he's got to ########
######## just know,

INSERT IN PAGE 6 after words: "What do we do for them Doc........
......He didn't answer me direct, but he casually inquired if I had
had a good season. I told him that outside of Waxahatchie, Texas,
Hershey, Pennsylvania, Concord, New Hampshire, and Newton, Kansas,
that I had got by in paying quantities.

42

to the phone again and called up. I couldn't think who they would be
calling now, they already had the doctor and the surgeon. I says "The
only other man who can possibly work with these is the undertaker".
But I was relieved to hear that it was only the hospital he was calling.
He was asking for a nice room. "Yes, we will be there in the morning,"
he says. My wife says, "Doctor, is there any danger in this operation"?
Well, as bad as I felt I had to laugh at that. They remarked together
in unison(I think that's what you call call it when you both speak at
once, ain't it?)"why, there is just a half of one percent", as tho they
                     ABOUT
had rehearsed it. I thought to myself,"Those babys have pulled that one
many a time. "Half of one percent", I thought to myself. #That's the
chance people have got of taking a drink in this country, is half of
one percent. But look what happening". Of course my wife took them
seriously, and they were reaching for their hats and all smiling and
you would have thought we had all made a date to have some fun and go
hear Aimee preach. They said they would take me down to the hospital
and see how I got along. Well, after the Doctors had left that gave my
wife and I a chance to do a little thinking. What they had
talked a bout had scared the pains clear away. We got to wondering what
had brogght on this severe attact at this time. We laid it to everything
we could think of. Will Hatyes had just been out here and spent
the day with us. Now I don't lay the illness directly to him, but a continual listening to the merits of the Movies and the Republican Party
will sometimes react disastrously on a previously ailing stomach.

My wffe was setting on the edge of the bed and we were talking it
over and she got up and left, and I thought to myself, "Poor
Betty, she can't stand this, it's too much for her, she's gone
so I can't see her." I get up and go in to console her. She was
digging in an old musty leather case makked "Insurance Papers".
Well, the house hold was up bright and early next morning to get old
Dag #### off to the hospital. The whole place was what the novelist
might call agog. Even the chauffeur(part time) had the old car all
shined up. This going to a hospital was a new thing to me. I had
never been in one in my life only to see somebody else. Outside of
those flat iron episodes I had never been sick a day in my life.
I had been appearingon the stage some twenty odd years and had
never missed a show in my life, but I was going to make up for it now.
They were taking me to the Swedish Lutheran Hospital. I knew nothing
about it myself, it didn't make much difference I was cut under, but
the reason we went there Lindberg was at his heighth at that time, and
I felt like out of respect to him we ought to make it a Swedish year.
We went right in. A hospital is the only place you can get in without
having baggage or paying in advance. They don't hold the trunk like a
hotel, they just hold the body. They had an awful pretty oozy room.
The whole thing was like a big hotel, and I thought I was in the wrong
place because I couldn't smell Iodoform. Everything was jolly and
laughter. The stomach had quit hurting of course. Did you ever have
a tooth hurt after you got to a dentist? I couldn't see any use of
going to bed at ten o'clock in the morning when I hadn't been out the
night before. Then in comes the nurse. WOW! #######################
############################### ################## I got one
look at her and made it continuous. They introduced her as 'Miss'. She
was Ziegfeld's front row without a dissenting vote.

I got one look at Mrs. Rogers, who was looking her over also, and
then says, "Doctor is this operation necessary"? I spoke up ahead
of the doctor and said, "I am beginning to think it is". Then I
thought to myself, If this girl is this good looking and still single
she has let all her patients die, for if one ever got out alive them
would have nailed onto her. Oh, yes, I like to forgot to tell you,
during this time I was turning yellow. (That is one of the symptons
of the Gall is that it produces Jaunders) Well, the doctors were both
remarking"very yellow, he is getting yellower, aha!" They didn't
know it but I wanted to tell them that yellow was from the heart, and
not from the liver and the gall bladder. They gave instructions what
to do to get me ready for tomorrow. I didn't think I had any getting
ready to do only just to furnish the stomach. Besides I had never
believed much in a reprieve. Then I thought maybe the surgeon wants
to practice a little in the meantime. Well, the hilarity was at its
height. You'd have thought there was going to be a picnic at the hospital the next day. But I did feel funny, great big old hundred
and eighty pound lummox having women fussing around with him when you
didn't seem like you needed them. But later on I was mighty glad to
have them to do something I tell you. The night nurse was also a
very pleasant cheerful fine capable little woman. Things were going
along fine around the hospital, but up around the old Rogers Igloo
things were stirring. The night before the operation Mrs. Rogers got
to studying "Now these two men just came in here and they say there ###
should be an operation. Of couse I know they are capable and fine men.,
The best doctors to be secured on the Western Coast, but I just wish
I could get some more advice." In the meantime she gets hold of
Mary Pickford who lives on the expensive end of the same hill, and
has a very widely seen house. Betty thinks Mary is mighty smart,

45

In fact everybody that knows Mary has that single-tract thought.
She knew Mary must have a pretty good doctor for she had been able
to keep Dough jumping ## all these years without any operation, and
maybe he can do something for my handsome Douglas. Mary's doctor
was out of town(I should have said 'City', that's what the Chamber of
Commerce advises us to say in speaking of Los Angeles). But she knew
another one, and told my wife about it. She got him. You see Betty
got to thinking, after all the shooting was over that I was down in the
hospital waiting to be operated on, " Now there's old Will , while he
hasn't been a good husband, he's done about the best he could and knew
how. While he's been funny to some people, he has at times been sad
to me. But as ornery as he is I'm not going to give him up without
a struggle". You see she had, during our years of association with
stage and screen people, seen so many second husbands who hadn't even
turned out to be
been as good as the first, that it set her wondering. Then our old
friend Bill Hart called up. He had a fine doctor that he wanted her to
talk to and see me. So she asked our two if they minded her having
these other two look me over, and all confer. Well, they of couse
didn't, and they knew it would make her feel better to have more
opinions on it, and they felt that their case would stand up before
witnesses. She made them promise that they wouldn't operate the next
morning until they had held this fourseome over my fairway. All the
                                                all
time they were going right ahead getting me ##ready. The night before
they wrapped my stomach all up in a bandage. I guess that was so
no doctor could get at it ahead of them. Then there was a batallion
of blood experts. Every few minutes there would be #### a girl come
in dressed like a manicurist and carrying a manicure set, and say,
"Hold out your left hand". Well, I wouldn't know whether she was
going to wash it, kiss it, hold it, or bead it. She would take a
sharp knife and take the tip end of one finger and cut it and get the

blood and put it in a cute little container. I would just get
settled down to steady worrying again when in would pop another
one. She wanted the same thing only a different finger. Finally
one came in after all the fingers had been tapped and I said "Good
joke on you, there aren't any left", but she kept right on acoming
and grabbed me by the ear, the same way we do when we are going to
year down a bronc to get a hackamore on him. She just slit the lower
end of the heavy set ### part of my ear. I told her my ear marks used to
be "drop and split the right, and underslope the left". I didn't tell
her ## tho that we also dew-lapped 'em. I says, "Is there some particular
brand of blood that you get from the ear that perhaps wouldn't go in
any other locality." She smiled sweetly, rolled up my ear's her blood in a
tube, and says, "Thank you". Well, by then I was growing weak
from loss of blood. I got so every time a girl would come along
with a tray I would start holding out my hands or my ears. I began
to think that some of them were keeping a friend that might be anemic.
The next morning after what should have been breakfast, but I didn't
get any as they won't operate on a full stomach, neither will a bull
fighter fight a cow. Well in filed the batallion of doctors. Betty
was with them. One says, "He is yellow". Then each of the others
repeated, "Yes". One of the new ones would ask a question and before
I had a chance to answer why one of my original cast in so many fewer
words than I could would explain. They listened and they thumped
the same as the first ones did. They discussed it all between
themselves. I, the defendant, wasn't put on the stand at all. Finally
they filed out. Imagine your life in the hands of a quartette, I'd as
soon trust a tenor. I wanted to get a chance to instruct the jury,
but nothing doing. The clinic was over. The nurse and I were left
alone. Betty had gone out too. I says, "How long do you

think the jury will be out,"?and do you think there is any chance of a disagreement"? A hung jury was the best I could hope for. I knew a verdict in my favor was out of the question. I could see by the way they acted that the doctor profession was a kind of a closed corporation, and while they might be professional rivals they wouldn't purposely knock each other out of anything. I asked the nurse again how she thought things would turn out. She said", Oh, they have the operating room engaged, they will have to go thru with it now". "Well," I said, "I had better go ahead then for I certainly don't want to cancel an operating room. Those people up there are going to be all broken up if I don't come up and be all cut up. But I wonder if there is not someone that would like a nice operation, and I could send them up in my place. There was a knock on the door and the jury came in. It stood four for operation. /In fact five, for

poor Betty they had won her over with tales of the advantages of
neat
a nice ^ operation. I knew the minute they opened the door that I had lost, for they all came in a smiling, and said"you are going to feel fine when this is over". I thought"yes, it depends on how I have lived, where I will finish when this is over". Well, it is customary I have heard for the defendant to shake hands with the

jury, but that's only in cases of acquittal. So they all went out and forgot to shut the door and I heard my two bidding the other two good bye, and thanking them and saying, "We'll do as much for you sometime boys". My surgeon stepped back into the room with his Vassar graduating gown on. That shows you the verdict was framed before hand, for they must have had those suits on under their others. Oh, they were tickled to death. They being golfers you would have thought they had broken a hundred and ten. Well, I saw right away that they were going to make me a hole-in-one. The main old carver said he had a lot of other operations that day but that mine would be first . I asked him if he couldn't take

somebody else first, that there might be someone in pain and that
I never had felt better in my life. Then I thought his hand might
be a little shakey early in the morning. They put a pair of what
looked like flannel boots that came pretty nearly up to the knee.
They looked like these gouleshes these girls wear in the winter when
they don't fasten the buckles and they come down the street sounding
like a mule that's broken loose with chain harness on. I never did
find out what those boots were on me for, unless it was to catch the
blood in case you got up and run out , or to keep you from biting
your toe nails, in case you got nervous during the operation. I didn't
have any kind of a shirt or night gown on. I had a sheet kind of
draped over me. All I needed was my hands crossed. They tied a white
thing around my head. All I needed was Klan card. The doctor had a
thing over his mouth so he wouldn't catch the same disease I had.
Bill Hart, bless his old heart, was there. He, like any good sports-
man,
wanted to be in at the death. I was on the wagon and all ready.
We were waiting signlas from the operating room. Betty, God bless her,
over
zame over to hold my hand. I told her to go #### and hold the surgeons
for the next thirty minutes
hand and we would all be safe . Then we got the signal that we #
######## were next. You never saw such hustling around. They
seemed to think, "Do you realize there's not a sould in this place
being whittled on at this minute". I bid good bye to Betty and the
hall
parade started down the ### and to the elevator. We passed another
wagon ##### ######## that had just come down with an old boy on
it.##### I wondered how he had made it. Then I heard him cussing, and
I thought he's all right, and even if he ##### passes out he will
have the satisfaction of telling them what he thought of them before
he left.

As I am rol ing to the operating room with a retinue of Nurses
and Doctors as outriders, I thought I ought to pull some kind of
a Gag when I get in there that will get a laugh, *THERE IS THIS*
~~By this time we are in the~~ room, I had never seen one before,
there was kind of a little balcony up above the floor, Where people
with a well developed sense of humor could sit there and see other
people cut up, It must be loads of fun. But there wasent a soul
in there then, I thought well *HERE* I ~~certainly~~ am palaying meby my last act,
to *AN EMPTY HOUSE* ~~the greatest house keeping if would be possible to have.~~
There was a lot of Doctors and more nurses than I ever saw in my
life, One was there ~~so~~ they told me afterwards just to ~~count the~~ *furnish*
~~packs of gauze they put in you to absorb the blood,~~ Then she counts *COUNT EVERY SINGLE THING USED*
~~up when the operation is over and it all got tobbbbbbbbb they have it~~ *INSIDE YOU DURING THE OPENING*
~~taken them out and they have to be correct, how done~~ before there is *EVERY CAUSE PACH HAS TO TALLY BE-ACCOUNTED FOR*
any sewing up, ~~the Docyd counts on everything that goes in and its~~
~~nothing more very than so eliminate all these stories article stories,~~
so she removes *s* most of the humor from opearations by making it *FOR YOUVSKF*
impossible to ~~tell~~ what w asleft inside. *YOU*
One fellow had a kind of a hose ar angement with a a ███ a nozzle
████ on it, Well I had by this time thought of my Gag and
I was already to pull it and set the whol place in agood natured *UTTER*
uproar, I just opened my mouth to my comical wheeze when this old
hose boy just gently spli pped that nozzle right over my nose and
mouth both, I wanted to tell him just a minuete" and I went to reach
up to snatch it off and a couple of men who had enlisted as
interns but in reality were wrestlers on a vacation, had me by each
hand, And I was so sore, here I had this last aprting "Wisecrack%%"
and it had been snuffed out before I could give vent to it, And
what made it so bad, do you know to this day I cant think of what

50

IT
~~twas~~ was, I remember at the time I thought it was going to be a
KNOCKOUT *REMEMBER ST...*
~~good time~~, But I just cant ~~think what it was.~~

The ~~gas~~ and the Ether just completely knocked it into another world,

You see the first thing they bump you off with is Gas, that puts you

where you wont tell any bum gags, Then they give you the Ether, that

is the Post graduate course in knockout drops, When you get that you

dont even leave a call, I just knew this old boy was a smothering me

but there was nothing I could do about it, I would have minded him

smothering me so much but there was a fellow commenced to hammering

and drilling a hole through the side of the hospital, and they kept

right on pounding and drilling right toward my head, Then the Birds

started singing, But they only sang a minute ~~for some fellow without a~~

~~made up like a bear playing a saxophone, it wasent in tune, Oh it was~~

~~terrible, and it drove the birds away, I was wishing for the Birds~~

when we had a shipwreck, and everybody on the boat was ~~gping~~ going down and

it looked like they were trying to push me under, Then a Farmer
                                                    relief
started running hollering for ~~help~~, anda fellow shot him to put him out
                                                    craziest
of his mortgages, Then there was a hall full of the ~~funniest~~ looking

people, and a man would read off some numbers for one man and then

he would raed them for another, and would say there wasent enough
                        they had just agreed when the w- come to an e-
to nominate, and the thing went on for a month, and ~~then the world come~~
                running   ~~(to an end,~~
Another fellow was a /hollering I dont Choose to run, and all the time

he was ~~just a flying and laughing to himself,~~ *RUNING FASTER*

THAN ANYBODY

Then I was in a bus trying to make grade crossing , and as you know the
trains never run fast till they get near a crossing, and it was right on us
when the Chinese started sheeling the town and saying "We are Missionarie
and you will have to worship Budda, and go to the mission schools and learn
Chinese" Then the Nicaraguans started drop ing Aeroplane Bombs on us, we
couldent do anything but let em drop, they said they wanted to protect
the Unites Sttaes as they wanted to put a canal through here some time"
Then I was rehersing with the Follies and Coolidge and I was ~~doing&&&&&&~~
~~&&&&&&&&&~~ working togeather, We had an act framed up where we had
asked an Englishman to dissarm , and he strted laughing and we couldent
get him stopped, and we had to ring down the curtain, Then the water kept
rising till it got up around the bed, and there was women and children and
horses and mules and Levees and cotton Gins and Aeroplanes and boats, and
a fellwo got up ina great hall full of men and said," We cant pass this
bill it will take too much ~~of&the&&&people~~ money, If its passed the
income ~~&&&~~ tax cant be lowered". Then another crevasse broke, and we
were all drowing when I heard the Nurse on one side and My Wife on the
other both saying,"You are all right, lay perfectly still, You are fine
now" " "Just lay perfect;y still and just relax" How was I going to do
anything else, wasent every bone in my body broke, wasent my throat cut,
hadent I remembered falling off that high building, " You will be allright
you are fine, Just relax and go back to sleep". " Yes dear its all over
and you are fine, " said my betty, whats fine I dont see anything fine
dident the Airship burn up and me right in it, " The Doctors are right
here, Dear" My Lord have I gota Re-take". " Just be quiet now"
If this is what they call saving anybody, what did they save me for?.
~~&&&&&&&&~~. " Its the ether", No its not the ether, its me, I know
what I am doing, I am dying and you all are just standing there while - do it
Damm, the whole gang of you.

Finally this ether got to leaving me and I sorter remembered what the
thing had been for, I asked em, " Did you get any stones"?, Gall
I was interested in the quality and the Karats, I thought they might find
something unusual, For any stone that hurt me that bad must have had corners
on it, I figured it must be a rough diamond.
"Yes they had gotten some, a couple of sizable dimensions, But nothing in
anyway approaching what could be worthy of exibition purposes,
I felt right then that the opeartion had been a failure, Whats the use
of having one of you couldent show something worth talking about.
I then asked, " Did you take out the Gall Bladder"?, He had told me he
might jarr me loose from that particular organ, " No," They said, " We
found a condition there that was unusual, and it warranted us not taking
it out%%%%%% at this time, But WE had found it and if at any time
I ever had any more trouble with it why it would be no trouble to go in
and get IT", "Oh" I says "you found out hwre it was, This operation was
in the nature of exploitation, or research, "ell I am glad you located it
anyway,", but suppose in my jumping around the country the way , do
trying to find a Democrat what if this thing should change its
SPOT, Its liable to be here today gone tomorrow,

     I would keep seeing the Doctors and also the Nurse
keep looking down on the floor at the side of my bed, I thought at
first it was a dog under the bed, They would frown and look worried and
then move away, I says "Whats under there thats causing all the
mysterious peesp, "?, She sid " Thats the drain from the tubes"?
Drain from what tubes?, " Why the tubes that are in you%% SIDE The doctor
put THEM IN Lord I thought they opened me up to take
out things not to put in, You talk like their might be a series of them
in there how many is there if its a fair question?, She lo ked and
counted em and said "two".

"Two, I was hoping there was more than that, You can never get much
distance on one of those two tube sets, We had one at home in Beverly
and all we could ever get would be, " Praise the Lord, Make it a
good collection, God loveth a cheerful giver", It was a womans voice.

All I thought my goodness, I am nothing but an old casing with
a couple of inner tubes in me. Well all this worry of the Doctors
was from the fact that I wasent draining, They had found a rather
"Unusual" condition in there, (being in California it would be UNUSUAL)
The Main Duct, (Now I am going to get into some techmical stuff
here, thats it only people who have had the advantages of superior
operations will understand, So the riff raff better ship over this
part, its only for the Intelligencia, You know there is nothing
broadens one like an opeartion.) You see I spoke of Duct, now to you
ordinary boneheads, Duct is the thing a batter does when the pitcher
throws one too close to his bean, Well I dident have sense enough to
know it but I was in pretty bad shape, For this drain was over
two days and nights showing up, It seems it wasent due to defective
plumming but there was some sort of a stoppage in the mian duct that
comes down out of the Liver, Well the Doctors slept right there at the
hospiatl, They was trying everything from Gluecose to Murphys drip,
As bad as I felt I could tell that something wasent breaking just right,
Things were looking bad for Claremore Oklahoma's favorite light
light-headed Comedian. If things dident show up pretty soon it looked
like I had annoyed my last President. Betty was a better actor than the
Doctors she hid it better than they did, Finally it showed up, and Dr
Moore got one look and sh outed, " If I was a drinking man, I would try
some of my own prescriptions tonight/" He was so tickled that I
believe if I had paid my bill then I would have got 50 percet off.
I says dont go use one of your own, and I may be the means of
saving your life.

He then tells me what shape I have been in, and he sits down and
takes a pad out of his pocket and drws a ~~diagram~~ blue print of the whole thing,
(thats one thing any Californian can do is draw a Blue print, showing
you where in six months there will be three bansks, a subway and
Marshall field store right next to your lot he is trying to sell you.
THE MAIN DUCT — ETC —
So here is what he drew as well as I can remember, " There is a
right lobe and a left lobe of the liver,a good deal depends on which
side the trouble is on, If you eat more on the right side of the
mouth why the trouble is libale to be in the right lobe, and visa
versa, The ~~llverlllllllllllllllll~~ map started in with the liver
~~llllll~~ as that was the north boundry of my trouble, What lays north
of that I have no idea, it may be the Thorax or the Medulla Oblong
gota, Now just below and sorter around the corner in what the oil
men w ould call an offset, && near the termination of the wishbone is a
small sort of a pocket, ~~the~~ you know the liver is shaped kinder
like a boxing glove and where it laces up is whre the big duct
strts in, This little pocket is not very large, you wouldent hardly
notuce it if stones didnt get crosswise in in its main entrance,
Its called the gall bladder and is sahped kinder like hot dog,
maby one that has been stuffed more at one end than the other.)
Now this main duct that runs from the liver south into the stomach
runs by this little hot dog stand, and there is abranch line that taps
into this minature jewel case, Now thats the little alley that gets
clogged up, of course he had dug it out, but tha mian line above duct
was the one that wasent hitting, *WITH ME* No stome vold be up there for a
stone wont go up hill, Well he explained it so nice ; wa s sorry
I hadent taken up doctoring for it seemed so easy, "e left me the ~~plat~~ *MA*
AND he had written it on the same piece of paper he had kept his Golf
score, so I dont know now whether he went from the liver into t

the mian duct in par, or if he took threes on the green, I could tell

from the drawings that he~~w~~ was in the rough when he hit the ~~will~~ *LITTLE*

DUCT
~~bladder~~, The drawing looked like he had taken about three Noblicks

and two putter mashies to get on the fairway d~~o~~n into the stomach.

Then I would get the nurse to draw out what she thought had happened,

Course she would have the liver on the opposite side and maby be

shaped like bonnett, But I ~~xxxxxxxxxxxxxxxxxxxxxxxxx~~ just thought if
was
everybody ~~is~~ shaped as different on the inside as they are on the
ANYBODY MIGHT MAKE A MISTAKE
a womans
outside, a Doctor wouldent know whether whether to cut into ~~your~~ Hip ~~is~~
the waist where her
or your shoulder to find ~~xxxxxxxxx~~stomach.was,

Taks a long tall fellow, his interior furnishings must all be draped

up and down, while witha lit le dumpy short Bird they must lay

horizontal, The doctor showed me a sword there that he operates on very

fat people with. and a slender person if they want in the ceter of

them they can go in either side bcak or front, Just whuch ever way they

happen to be laying when the doctor arrives , he opens them witha

a safety razor, Operate ona slim ones with safety razor so they wont
go through,
Then I had the nurse go to the Hospital Library and get me all the

books on this locality, showing the interior in colored Photography,

it looked like Cecil Demille movie, *AND THE WAIST...*
SUPPOSE SHE SAYS...
Now the gall goes into this little resepticle and remains till needed *UNDER MY WAIST...*

that is till you get sore at somebody and want to use eup some on them,

thts why it is the good natured people that have gall operations they

never have cáuse to use any of it, Another thing I learned is that the
~~gall bladder~~
complaint is more common by far among women than men, Well that fac

made me feel rather effiminate.

Now as I have thoroughly explained the location of it, what cause

the stone to form,?Well there is various reasons, Republicans staying

in power too long will incre ase the epidemic, Seeing the same ending

ending to Moving Pictures is aprime cause, A Wife driving from the rear
seat will cause Gastric Juices to form an acid that slowly jells into
a stone as she keeps hollering,

Of course I will always ~~claim that~~ believe that mine was caused by
no Sanitary drinking cups in the old Indian Territory where I was born,
We used a goard, raised from a goard vine, Not only did we all drink
out of the one goard, but we drank out of the same one till prohibition
weaned us away from water. Then our handkerchiefs might have had
something to do with it, we just bought them all togeather, not done up
in a seperate little paper container at all, some clerk might of had
Gall trouble and slipped it to me that way, Then sometimes about all we
had to polish our teeth with was the rib of a yearling heifer,
I believe if these modern sanitary methods hadent come in that by now
four out of five would have had Gall stones,

     however
A funny thing ~~though~~ I dident find out till about ten days after the
operation, was ~~what~~ just what caused mine personally, ~~the~~ I happened to
think of it, For years I have carried a very big, (that is big for my
circumstances) accident and sickness dissability insurance,
Well I would notice that my Wife would get a little nervous irritable every
year when it would come time to pay the premiums on these particular
policies, " Well thats pretty large to carry, aint it when you never
have got a cent out of it". and I would admit that it did seem like
like a bad investment, It was getting terribly disscouraging to pay year
after year for something you wasent getting and seemed no prospects of ever
receiving. Here I was betting a lot of large insurance Companies that I
would get sick or hurt and they was betting me that I wouldent, Now if
you think you are not a sucker in a case like that all you have to do
is to look at the financial standing of the Companies in comparison to th
people who bet on the other side, Its a cse of somebody knowing more

its a cse of somebody ~~lese~~ ELSE knowing more about you than you know
yourself, Why they have the highest priced Doctors just to look at
you, ~~and so he can told how tough you~~ are, If you look like nothing
but lightning can kill you, why he sends in a report to the Company to
bet you hat that you wont get sick. and if you look the least bit like you
are going to get sick ~~anyhow~~ he advises them not to bet you, anytime
they approve you that should show you right there that there is nothing
ever going to happen to you, But you like afool go ahed and bet them
in the face of all this proffessional knowledge, that you know more
than they do, I argued with my Wife "well I may be get sick and all
we got is my salary and this extra would help out". " Yes you might
get sick but you never do,". Well you see she had me licked, I then
said, "I might get hurt in a polo game by falling off my horse,"
she said " No you have fell off so much you got used to it, so I
have no more hpppes along that line.".

 So last summer when paying time come her and my Insurance man,(he
really shouldent be one because he alos advised her to reduce the
policiees) they decided to cut down on the accident and Dissability, But
they allowed the strainght life to remain, They let the death one ride
as they figured, if I dided it would be without illness, You see they
were a little more uncertain about my dying than about my being able t
live through an accident or sickness. well I dident knw the thing had
be n cut down till I was laying on the bed in the hospital one day and
I just happened to ~~think~~ have the only bright thought that I had ha
in weeks, " Say this thing that I am doubled up here with comee under
the h4ading of Sickness, It evens comes under the heading of accident ,
for wasent I getting well froma an opeartion,
So that brought on more thoughts of these Policies that I had been
been paying on for years, I ~~began~~ thought by golly the old sickness

58

is turning out good at that. I begin to think how I could stetch this
out into what might be termed a slow convalesence.

So I was a grinning like Moving Picture producer who has just thought of
a sugestive Title for haas picture,So when my wife called again I broke
the good news to her,&I&&&&&&&&&&&&&&&&&&&&&&&&&&&&&&&&&&&&&&&&&&&&
&&&&&&&&&& I says if we can get a boni fide Doctor to say that I have &&
been sick and couldent spin a rope and talk about Coolidge% why we are
in for some dis ability Well I noticed the wife dident fall for the idea
as boisterious as I had, Then I got to thinking well maby I havent
been sick or maby I havent gota boni fide Doctor, Then thetruth
slowly did %out, she told me the "y physical condition had missled them,
                                   sad story of the cut ing down, It read
like a sentence to me, Of course she said there would be some
salvage out of &&& our shortsightedness, but that the opeartion would
be by no means money making, when if the original policies had prevailed
I would have reaped a neat benefit, So if you want to stay well just
bet some rich Company you will get sick, Then if you cant have any
luck getting sick have the policy cut down, and you will be &&&&&&&&&&&
&&&& saying, "Doctor the pain is right there,"
Course &&&& I got this consolation, If I had had the bigger policy why
it would have had some clause in there where I got sick on the wrong
day,or had the wrong disease, that the policy dident cover rock quaries,
there would have been a an ~labi somehwre; fpr all those four pages of
clauses are not in there & just to make it longer, So I guess
                                       Its not the opeartion m butb
everything happens for the best anyway, castor oil afterwards, LOOK UP,

     &&&&&&&&&&&&&&&&&&&&&&&&&&&&&&&&&&&&&&&&&&&&&&&&&&&&&&&&&
&&&&&&&&&& Now I think anybody that suffers must do so witha view in mid
and any article should have a purpose, this article was not just written
to show you the wonderful human pictures that Herbert Johnston can draw,
this idea is bigger than art itself, When people have tosils removed

they   come out bargging about it, and tell what the opartion was for,
the same with adanoids, and Apendicibis they tell about their apendix
before you can get the cpcktails mixed, But with gall bladder they
never bring the nma eof the opeartion into public eashot, They say
they have ben operated on , but they dont say for what,

      Now 1 have figured out that it is the name thats against it,
Now ⸗ dont know why ~~the~~ ~~Gall bladder~~should be a more offensive thing
to speak of while the company is just settling down to steady scandal
gossip than any other part of the body,
                    a
Its just among ⸌lot of ⸜⸜⸜⸜ other what   they call organs, and tó
operate on these with undesirable names should be no disgrace for
                al
conversation/ purposes, But you see its just human nature, we always
like something with ⸜⸜⸜ some big name that we dont know anything abott
Some Doctor for no reason at all outside of the fee called it
Apendix it had a nice sounding name, Now everybody that dont know
what to be opearted on for have the apendix removed, Now the Gall
Blad⸌er means something, its a real name of a real functioning organ,
& the same as the heart functiones,(in some people) Its too sudden,
its crude, its not euphonius, Its like a tooth pick we want to ~~speak~~
~~of it~~ behind a handkerchief, And as for opeartion, why Apendix cant
compare with this other ----,----. Why Apendixes are taken out just
while they are looking for something else, just as akind of a by
play, while ----,-----, that calls for a table and a lot of girls
and a bunch of ether, Its a Surgeons opeartion while Apendix is a
nightwatchmans job, We have to change the name, and 1 suggest somethig
from the latin, People are crazy over Latin now since the Eucharistic
Conference in Cⱪicago, when the Americans couldent undetrstand a thing the
Cardinals said, The name Gaul is ~~allright we just change the spelling,~~
Gaul was a nation that flourished, when flourishing was good, and were
extinguished when the extinguishing was good, Its the word Blad er that

60

AQUATIATIS, GeeBee's, Not HeeBee JeeBee's, But just GeeBee's
we object too, zo we change it to the latin word Reseptacle, and call
it "Nerve reseptible", that name will give us antree into any crowd,
I dont want to just stand arounda crowd and point to my scar and not
be able to tell what / put it there, Ours is higher up that this
Apenix gagng and we can point to it with more pride modesty,

All operations should be on an equality, any time you have
whiffed the ther that makes you eligible to speak publically and call
your operation bty name, no mater what they remodelled or took out, if
you have been overhauled you should be able to enter any converstaion,
for you are then one of the fraternity of SCARBELLIES?
So if I can lift the GeeBee operation to a social standing in
conversational circles that Apendix is why then my illnes will not hae
been in vain,

NOTES

[1] In this first paragraph of the *SEP* article, Putnam's deleted the following: *This is a serial in two parts. You may be one of those who don't like continued stories. But this fact might interest you:* . . .

[2] Irvin S. Cobb (1876-1944) was a writer, friend, and fellow humorist who knew Will Rogers well. Cobb also wrote a number of movie scripts in which Will starred. Here Rogers refers to Cobb's book *Speaking of Operations*.

[3] Putnam's deleted the following: *I had tried to crowd all this cause and effect of this operation into one Article, or Installment. Then I got to thinking about the bill—it hadent come yet. But I knew my literary efforts were not appreciated enough by hard-hearted Editors to have one installment pay for a modern, up-to-date, with all late improvements operation.*

[4] George Bernard Shaw (1856-1950), the famous British author, was invited to a stag dinner held for Will Rogers in London while Will and his family were visiting England. Thus, Will had met Shaw and had the opportunity to exchange jokes and witticisms with him.

[5] The *SEP* version read: *But I decided on two parts, and if its not humorous* . . .

[6] Edward Clarence Moore (1882-1944) was a well known surgical specialist and physician in the Los Angeles area, and later, a clinical professor of surgery at the University of Southern California. Percival Gordon White (1881-1942) was a specialist in internal medicine and, as Doctor Moore's partner, aided the surgeon in the diagnosis of Will's gallbladder problems and the subsequent operation.

[7] Will was born near Oologah, and always planned to retire in Eastern Oklahoma. The Verdigris river drains the area and is part of the navigation system of the first inland port of Catoosa, near Tulsa.

[8] The SEP version read: . . . *Cheatam's Chill Tonic* . . .

[9] Gilda Gray (c. 1898-1959) (Marianna Michalaska) was a Polish dancer who became popular in America during the 1920's. She worked with Will Rogers in the Ziegfeld Follies, where she is credited with inventing the "shimmy." Here Rogers refers to her dancing technique.

[10] The *SEP* version: . . . *Jublio./*The Plot Begins to Thicken/*It hadn't shown* . . . "Jublio" was one of Roger's first feature length photoplays, based on the story by Ben Ames Williams and produced by Goldwyn Pictures Corporation, 1919.

[11] The *SEP* text reads: . . . *until this spring* . . .

[12] Calvin Coolidge (1872-1933), President of the United States (1924-1928), often was the subject of Will's comments in his daily telegrams and weekly articles. Once on radio Will imitated Coolidge, bringing approval from the president but criticism from many people who thought Rogers was Coolidge. Will was very sorry he had caused such a response, and never again imitated Coolidge in a way to fool an audience.

[13] Aimee Semple McPherson (1890-1944), an evangelist, founded the International Church of the Foursquare Gospel. Preaching a Pentacostal, fundamentalist, faith healing doctrine, she toured the world beginning in 1916. Will made numerous references to her and her public and private antics.

[14] Will Hays (1879-1954) was an American executive and a power in Republican politics. He served as president of the Motion Picture Producers and Distributors Association of America (1922-1945) and authored its high-toned Production Code (1930). His efforts to improve the medium and create a new image after the Roscoe "Fatty" Arbuckle scandal and the death of Wallace Reid are detailed in his *Memoirs* published in 1955.

[15] Charles A. Lindbergh (1902-   ), pioneer aviator who accomplished spectacular flying feats, toured Mexico with Will Rogers in the 1920's at the request of United States Ambassador Dwight W. Morrow. Lindbergh's grandfather had been born in Sweden in 1810, and became Secretary to King Charles XV. Hence Rogers' reference to a Swedish hospital.

[16] Florenz Ziegfeld (1869-1932), a theatrical producer, began his career as promoter of musical features for the Chicago World's Fair, 1893. His musical revue, the "Follies", noted for lavish settings and the attractive chorus types, was introduced to the United States in 1907 and became highly successful for the next twenty years. Will Rogers, with W. C. Fields, Eddie Cantor and hundreds of other entertainers, performed for Ziegfeld.

[17] Mary Pickford (1893-   ) (Gladys Smith) was a Canadian actress, who, in the heydey of silent films, became known as "the world's sweetheart." Retired, the widow of Douglas Fairbanks whom she married in 1920, her home has been for many years a major attraction for those who visit Hollywood. She was co-founder of United Artists Films and one of America's richest women. Rogers refers to her widely respected business ability.

[18] Douglas Fairbanks (1883-1939), one of the most popular stage stars during the era before movie making and the first to realize the shift of early films toward highly romantic material, was known for his athletic prowess on screen. Rogers refers to this ability.

[19] William S. Hart (1870-1946) began his acting career on the stage in 1889, entering the movies in 1914, where he became the solemn-faced Western hero of the silent screen and made scores of some of the most realistic films to be produced, before retiring in 1926. A close friend of Will Rogers, it was Hart who spoke at Occidental College while Will was hospitalized.

[20] Will made numerous comments about missionaries seeking new fields in the Orient, and on Nicaraguan attitudes toward the United States and attempts to build a canal in Nicaraguan territory.

[21] Rogers is commenting on flood victims in Mississippi. He often donated his time appearing at benefits for these people.

[22] Cecil B. De Mille (1881-1959), in films from 1913, was noted for his scenes in society sex dramas and pseudo-biblical spectacles. His innovations in movie making made him one of America's foremost producer-directors.

[23] Eddie Cantor (1892-1964) (Edward Israel Isskowitz), on stage from New York childhood, became a Ziegfeld star in 1916, and from that time until the middle of the century his rolling eyes, sprightly movement and inimitable singing voice took him from vaudeville to motion pictures, radio and TV.

[24] Benito Mussolini (1883-1945), Italian political and military leader, began his rise to power in the 1920's. Rogers interviewed Mussolini in 1926. Here he refers to the Italian ruler's use of castor oil in interrogating political prisoners.

[25] In *SEP: . . . Moral in this article. This article was not just written to show you the wonderful human pictures that Herbert Johnson can draw; this idea is bigger than art itself. When people . . .*